The
Solo Stove
Fire Pit
Cookbook

The Solo Stove Fire Pit Cookbook

Fireside Food for Good Moments with Family and Friends

solo stove

An Official Cookbook

HARVARD
COMMON
PRESS

Quarto.com

© 2024 Quarto Publishing Group
USA Inc.
Text and photographs © 2024
Quarto Publishing Group USA Inc.,
except as otherwise indicated

Photographs © 2024 Solo Brands,
LLC, on pages 6–18, 26–27, 30, 34–
35, 40, 47, 62, 74–75, 84, 100–101,
126, 145, 149, 150–151, 160.

Solo Stove® and Solo Stove logos
are registered trademarks of Solo
Brands, LLC

First Published in 2024 by The Harvard
Common Press, an imprint of The
Quarto Group, 100 Cummings Center,
Suite 265-D, Beverly, MA 01915, USA.
T (978) 282-9590 F (978) 283-2742

The Harvard Common Press titles are
also available at discount for retail,
wholesale, promotional, and bulk
purchase. For details, contact the
Special Sales Manager by email at
specialsales@quarto.com or by mail at
The Quarto Group, Attn: Special Sales
Manager, 100 Cummings Center, Suite
265-D, Beverly, MA 01915, USA.

ISBN: 978-0-7603-9327-7

Digital edition published in 2024
eISBN: 978-0-7603-9328-4

Library of Congress Cataloging-in-
Publication Data available.

Design and layout: Burge Agency

Cover Image: Kelsey Foster
Photography

Photography: Kelsey Foster
Photography, except the following by
Shutterstock on pages 44, 52, 59, 69,
86, 93, 121, 137, and by Solo Stove
on pages 6–18, 26–27, 30, 34–35,
40, 47, 62, 74–75, 84, 100–101, 126,
145, 149, 150–151, 160.

Printed in China

To learn more about Solo Stove fire
pits, cooking accessories, and other
Solo Stove products, please visit
solostove.com

28 27 26 25 24   1 2 3 4 5

To our extraordinary Solo Stove family, whose unwavering dedication and creativity have shown us the endless possibilities that can be cooked up over the flames of our fire pits.

Contents

Introduction:
The Basics of
Fire Pit Cooking

Cooking over a crackling fire is an unmatched experience—surrounded by the open sky, enveloped in the beauty of the outdoors, it evokes a sense of tradition and nostalgia that can harken back to childhood. We believe that cooking outdoors not only creates amazing meals but also long-lasting bonds between friends and family. *The Solo Stove Fire Pit Cookbook* will introduce you to a wide assortment of recipes that are sure to become family favorites. Cooking with fire has unique variables that may take some time to master, but the more you cook over flame and coals, the better you'll get.

The Solo Stove Cooking System is an efficient, simple way to enjoy fire pit cooking and take it to a higher level than classic hot dogs or marshmallows on a stick. Solo Stoves burn hot—sometimes over 1200°F (649°C)—and are smokeless once the fire is going well, so food cooks quickly, and you won't reek of smoke after creating your snack or meal.

The first step to any fireside adventure—whether just enjoying the fire or cooking—is to read the manuals front to back before using the Solo Stove. You will find safety and setup instructions, including how to start a fire and care for your new stove.

The manuals for the griddle, grill, and wok include the correct method of seasoning the cast-iron accessories before use. This step is crucial for creating a nonstick surface and helps prevent rusting. A well-seasoned cast-iron pan or grill is forgiving and will last decades. Cast-Iron heats up slowly and retains the heat, which makes it ideal for preparing food over a fire pit; this feature means you have time to add wood, if needed, and keep cooking.

While your Solo Stove comes with a lot of built-in benefits, you may find additional tools handy. These include the following.

Infrared Thermometer: One of the most challenging aspects of fire pit cooking is controlling the temperature of the fire and cast-iron accessories. Using a laser-assisted infrared thermometer is a game-changer. You can check the temperature of the cast-iron surface and allow it to cool down so you don't burn your ingredients. Cast-Iron is an excellent material for which an infrared thermometer is used for accuracy because of emissivity—a measurement of a material's ability to emit infrared energy. The scale ranges from 0.00 (poor) to 1.00 (ideal), and cast-iron is between 0.6 and 0.7.

Heat-Resistant Gloves: Fires get hot, and you will place your cast-iron cooking surfaces over the Solo Stove after burning it for a while. Gloves are a must-have item for safety. Look for heavy-duty insulated gloves, preferably ones that reach well past your wrists and are at least heat-rated for up to 450°F (232°C).

Roasting Sticks: If you have ever had to clean up a sticky mess after making s'mores, you know it can take as long as it took you to cook and eat the s'mores. A set of high-quality, easy-to-clean roasting sticks, such as our own Solo Stove Roasting Sticks, are a must. These roasting sticks are made of durable, dishwasher safe 304 stainless steel and come in a set of four, with a convenient travel case. Cooking with roasting sticks is the simplest and easiest way to cook over an open fire. See pages 16 and 17 for loads of ideas of things you can cook with a set of sturdy roasting sticks. Of course, if you're in a pinch, wooden skewers can also be used—just make sure to soak them for 30 minutes first.

Cooking Accessories: You probably already have an assortment of kitchen tools for all your recipe needs, but cooking over a fire on cast-iron might require a few new items. Some tools to consider include extra-long tongs, metal spatulas, an internal probe thermometer, a metal slotted spoon, and brushes for sauces.

For safety, keep fire extinguishers classed for grease handy, or salt, to smother a grease fire. Never pour water on a grease fire because the burning grease will float on top, and the fire can spread. Always read the manuals that come with the Solo Stove or accessories to familiarize yourself with any specific safety concerns and follow outdoor burn rules, including the local permits and fire bans for your region.

Quick Tips

Once you've set up the Solo Stove, tried a few fires in it, and seasoned your cast-iron, you are ready to try your hand at cooking. Here are seven tips to ensure the experience ends with platefuls of delicious food.

1. Pick the right wood: The best firewood tends to come from fruit trees (think apple) or nut trees (like pecan). Hardwoods, like oak, often also make for excellent firewood. You may need to cut firewood to the correct size for your stove. Do not use charcoal briquettes. If using a pellet adapter for the stove, ensure the pellets are graded for cooking and not for heating when making food.

2. Plan ahead: The fire will need to burn for a while to create the coal bed required for cooking, so start early. It will take four or five reasonably sized logs to create good coals. You can gather all the recipe ingredients and prep in that time—about one hour—or just enjoy sitting around the stove. Have small pieces of wood stacked nearby that you can add if the heat drops too far while cooking. You don't want the flames too high; keep them at a few inches above the coals so your food doesn't burn.

3. Preheat your cast-iron accessories: The first recipe step is usually preheating your pot or pan when cooking on a regular stove inside the house. The same is true on the Solo Stove. Cast-Iron must preheat for about ten minutes before it is ready for food. Use an infrared thermometer to determine the right time to start cooking. If you don't have a thermometer, sprinkle a few drops of water on the pan or grill. If the water dances and spits, you can start cooking. For most recipes, except searing steak, the best range is between 350°F and 450°F (177°C and 232°C). To get a feel for how your Solo Stove works and how quickly it cooks, take it for a few test drives. We find that eggs make excellent test subjects, since you can try a single one at a time. Pancakes work well for testing, too.

4. Get familiar with hot spots: The center of the griddle, wok, or grill will be hotter than the outside edges. Fires aren't an even continuous heat source, and factors like how you stack the wood or the uneven height of the coal bed can influence the heat. You must watch the food carefully, moving it when necessary and flipping it a few more times than on a regular stove. Use these hot spots for your benefit; food can be moved to the edges for more indirect heat, especially when multitasking a meal. More delicate ingredients like vegetables or eggs can be prepared on the edges while you cook a steak or burger in the middle. Or wrap naan bread or tortillas in neat foil packets and set them near the edges to warm while preparing fish for tacos or chicken fajitas in the center.

5. Choose the right fat for cooking: Although well-seasoned cast-iron is nonstick, you still need oil for most ingredients or recipes to ensure the best results. A couple tablespoons usually do the trick to coat the surface. The best choices are oils with high smoke points, like canola, flaxseed, and avocado oil. Lower smoke point oils can heat up too fast and break down, which adds an unpleasantly bitter flavor to food. If you want to use butter, stick to lower-temperature cooking—its smoke point is 350°F (177°C)—and watch the process closely. Olive oil has a smoke point of about 410°F (210°C), so it is fine as long as you monitor your cooking surface with an infrared thermometer or cook near the edges.

6. Don't worry about perfection:
Is every dish you make on the
Solo Stove going to be a culinary
masterpiece? No. Learning this
cooking method is about embracing
trial and error, but even mistakes
can be delicious. Besides, all food
created around a fire with family
and friends tastes better, and the
memories—even of less than perfect
meals—are special. Your eggs might
get a bit overdone, perhaps your
bacon will be slightly more crispy
than ideal, and some items may
get a bit charred. No problem.
Charring is a natural part of cooking
over a fire; it does not mean your
food is burnt. The flavor added with
some charring can be enjoyable, so
don't stress.

**7. Clean and store the
accessories:** Follow the
recommendations in the manual
for safe and effective cool down
and cleanup of the Solo Stove
Cooking System. Let the cast-iron
accessories cool down naturally;
don't throw water on them, or they
will be damaged. When cool, wipe
them with a rag or paper towels,
and if they need further cleaning,
use a specially designed scrubber
or coarse salt. Wipe the surface
with a damp cloth to remove the
residue, then thoroughly dry the
accessory. You can apply a thin oil
coating before packing the cast-iron
into a cover to store until next time.
Visit solostove.com for a carrying
bag to store and transport cast-iron
accessories for the fire pit.

Everything these days seems to
be about quick convenience—
meal delivery apps, fast food,
drive-through lanes—so there
is something comforting and
rewarding about cooking a lovely
meal outdoors over a fire. You need
to be attentive and present in the
moment because food is done very
quickly over that heat; think of times
marshmallows on sticks caught
fire in an instant over a flame. But
the results are worth every effort.
Practice with the tempting recipes
in this book and tweak your favorite
home recipes to try on a griddle or
grill. Happy cooking!

Recipes

Cooking on a Roasting Stick

Solo Stove fires burn very hot so you may want to let the flames die down some, or hold the roasting stick a bit higher above the flames than you might have first thought, for the best results—and cooler fingers!

For more about types of roasting sticks, see page 9. Of course, if you're out in the wilderness and left your roasting sticks at home, you can always grab a stick and get cooking!

Apple or pear "pie": Peel an apple (or pear) and cut it into 2-inch (5-cm) chunks. Roll the chunks in melted butter, granulated sugar, and skewer them on roasting sticks. Sprinkle with cinnamon and roast over the fire until tender.

Bacon: Wrap a slice of bacon around a roasting stick and put it over the fire until sizzling and crispy. Brush the bacon with maple syrup or sprinkle with brown sugar to create a tasty variation.

Bread: Homemade or premade dough can be wrapped around a roasting fork or even the end of a broom and toasted over the fire until it is golden and cooked through. Don't wrap it too thickly, or the inside will be raw. Try using crescent roll dough or cinnamon roll dough and top it with a drizzle of icing or a dusting of sugar before eating.

Meat, chicken, pork, shrimp, or fish: Cook chunks of your favorite protein in bite-size pieces over a flame. Season with sauces, spices, or herbs and make sure poultry and seafood are cooked thoroughly.

Cheese: Cut any type of cheese (cheddar, Swiss, Asiago, Halloumi, Gouda) into 1½-inch (3.8-cm) chunks, thread onto your stick, and toast until just melty. You can also season the cheese with different oils, chili flakes, herbs, or spices before toasting. Serve with fruit or tucked between a few crackers.

Potatoes: Raw, small potatoes can be dipped in a melted butter and minced garlic mixture, and roasted until golden, crispy, and tender. Chunks of sweet potato can be dipped in butter, brown sugar, and cinnamon and roasted until lightly caramelized.

Sausages or hot dogs: Hot dogs are a traditional campfire treat, but you can expand into breakfast sausages, Oktoberfest sausages, and all other types. Just make sure they are cooked through or use smoked or cured products.

Fruit: Many kinds of fruit are truly spectacular when roasted. Try peaches, watermelon, pineapple, mangoes, nectarines, strawberries, or plums. They are delicious plain, sprinkled with cinnamon and brown sugar, or even dunked in marshmallow fluff.

Vegetables: Mushrooms, zucchini, peppers, cherry tomatoes, cauliflower, and butternut squash are all delicious roasted. Try them drizzled with olive oil and sprinkled with Parmesan before putting them over the heat.

1

Chapter 1

Fire Pit
Breakfasts

Servings:
2 people

Prep time:
10 minutes

Cook time:
4 minutes

Huevos Rancheros

Huevos Rancheros or rancher's eggs is a Mexican dish with salsa, beans, tortillas, and eggs. For this version, we serve the tortilla alongside the other fixings, but you can fold all the ingredients into a handheld wrap, too. If heat is something you enjoy, add some chopped jalapeños and a splash of hot sauce.

2 large (8-inch/20-cm) tortillas

1 tablespoon (15 ml) vegetable oil

4 large eggs

½ cup (86 g) black or pinto beans

½ cup (130 g) prepared or homemade salsa

¼ cup (60 g) sour cream

½ cup (58 g) shredded cheddar cheese

1 tablespoon (1 g) chopped fresh cilantro

1. Wrap the tortillas in a clean kitchen cloth and place them on the very edge of the griddle to warm (on the handle).

2. Add the oil to the center of the griddle and fry the eggs until the whites are set and the yolks are set to the desired firmness, about 4 minutes for still runny.

3. Place the tortillas on a clean work surface or serving plates and spoon ¼ cup (43 g) of the beans into the center of each, spreading them out a little.

4. Top each bean-covered tortilla with two fried eggs, ¼ cup (65 g) of salsa, 2 tablespoons (30 g) of sour cream, ¼ cup (29 g) of shredded cheese, and ½ tablespoon of cilantro.

5. Roll the tortillas up and serve immediately.

Servings:
4 people

Prep time:
10 minutes

Cook time:
5 minutes

Cooking Accessory:
Cast-Iron Griddle Top

Eggs in Bell Peppers

Egg rings are used in restaurants—and home kitchens—to make perfectly symmetrical sunny-side up eggs. Bell peppers stand in for the tool in this simple recipe. Make sure your peppers have a nice, wide diameter so there is room for the egg in the middle. You will be using beaten eggs because it can be difficult to cook the eggs through without overcooking the bottom otherwise.

1 tablespoon (15 ml) vegetable oil

2 large bell peppers (any color), cut into eight ½-inch-thick (1.3-cm) rings and seeded

8 large eggs

Sea salt, to taste

Freshly ground black pepper, to taste

1. Add the oil to the griddle and spread it with a spatula.

2. Arrange the bell peppers on the griddle with about 1½ inches (3.8 cm) between them and cook for 1 minute to lightly brown. Flip them over.

3. Meanwhile, in a small bowl, beat the eggs until well combined.

4. Divide beaten egg equally among the pepper slices, pouring the mixture into the center of each ring, and cook, stirring occasionally, until the eggs are set, about 4 minutes.

5. Season lightly with salt and pepper and serve two pepper ring eggs per person.

Servings:
2 people

Prep time:
10 minutes

Cook time:
12 minutes

Classic Steak and Eggs

You can find steak and eggs on most diner menus across North America, and in some fine-dining establishments, as well. Cooking everything on one handy griddle means no cleanup and a hearty meal in less than 30 minutes. The mushrooms and onions in this recipe ramp up the flavor, and if you're feeling super hungry, fry up some leftover cooked potatoes to round out the plate.

2 tablespoons (30 ml) vegetable oil

2 (6-ounce/170-g) striploin steaks, trimmed

Sea salt, to taste

Freshly ground black pepper, to taste

1 sweet onion, peeled and thinly sliced

1 cup (70 g) sliced cremini mushrooms

4 large eggs

1. Pour the vegetable oil on the griddle and spread it out with a spatula.

2. Season the steaks generously on both sides with salt and pepper.

3. Add the sliced onions and mushrooms to one side of the griddle and the steaks to the other.

4. Sauté the vegetables, stirring often, until they are tender and browned, about 8 minutes.

5. Cook the steaks, turning once, until the desired doneness, about 4 minutes per side for medium rare.

6. Transfer the steaks from the griddle to two serving plates and top them evenly with the onions and mushrooms.

7. Crack the eggs onto the griddle and cook them to the desired doneness, about 3 minutes for sunny-side up.

8. Transfer two eggs to each plate and serve.

Servings:
4 people

Prep time:
20 minutes

Cook time:
15 minutes

Cooking Accessory:
Cast-Iron Griddle Top

Root Vegetable Sausage Hash

Hash is just a mix of whatever ingredients you happen to have in your refrigerator, in this case, rich sausage meat, sweet root vegetables, and a fragrant blend of onions and garlic. Eggs and spinach round out this complex, and filling, dish. Feel free to substitute anything that suits your palate.

1 tablespoon (15 ml) vegetable oil

1 pound (450 g) ground lean sausage meat

1 sweet potato, peeled and shredded

2 carrots, peeled and shredded

2 parsnips, peeled and shredded

10 mini potatoes, halved

½ small sweet onion, thinly sliced

2 teaspoons (6 g) minced garlic

6 large eggs

1 cup (60 g) shredded spinach

Sea salt, to taste

Freshly ground black pepper, to taste

1. Pour the oil onto the griddle and spread it with a spatula.

2. Add the sausage meat and sauté until cooked through, about 6 minutes. Transfer the meat to a plate with a slotted spoon. Set aside.

3. Add the shredded vegetables, potatoes, onion, and garlic and sauté until the vegetables are browned and cooked through, turning frequently with the spatula, about 6 minutes.

4. Return the sausage to the griddle, tossing to combine, and push the hash to one side of the griddle. Crack the eggs onto the newly cleared side of the griddle. Cook, stirring often until soft, fluffy curds form and eggs are completely cooked, about 3 minutes. Combine the eggs and spinach with the hash and cook, stirring often, until the greens are wilted, about 30 seconds.

5. Serve seasoned with salt and pepper.

Servings:
2 people

Prep time:
5 minutes

Cook time:
10 minutes

Grilled Caprese Breakfast Sandwich

This dish is inspired by Insalata Caprese, a traditional salad that combines basil, tomatoes, and mozzarella. The salad is served as a starter but when you add bread and eggs, it becomes a filling breakfast. Look for fresh mozzarella whenever possible; it is worth the trouble.

2 large tomatoes, cut into ½-inch (1.3-cm) slices

2 (6-inch/15.2-cm) mini baguettes, sliced in half lengthwise

2 tablespoons (30 ml) vegetable oil, divided

4 large eggs

⅓ cup (60 g) prepared pesto

4 ounces (113 g) fresh mozzarella cheese, sliced into rounds

Sea salt, to taste

Freshly ground black pepper, to taste

1. Brush the tomato slices and the insides of the pieces of bread with 1 tablespoon (15 ml) of oil.

2. Arrange the tomato slices on one-third of the griddle and the bread cut-side down on another third. Brush the last third of the griddle with the remaining oil and crack the eggs.

3. Cook the tomatoes until warmed through, about 2 minutes per side. Transfer them to a plate.

4. Lightly toast the bread, about 2 minutes, and transfer it to a clean work surface. Evenly divide the pesto between the bread slices.

5. Fry the eggs until the whites are set and the yolks still runny, about 3 minutes. Evenly divide the eggs between 2 pieces of bread.

6. Evenly divide the mozzarella and the tomatoes between the two egg-covered baguette bottoms. Season lightly with salt and pepper and top the sandwiches with the remaining bread pieces. Serve hot.

Servings: Prep time: Cook time:
4 people 20 minutes 20 minutes

Grilled Breakfast Pizza

Pizza for breakfast! And not cold leftover slices in a delivery cardboard box. You can cook the sausage and mushrooms ahead and store them in an airtight container until you're ready to make this recipe. The trick to a perfect, crispy crust is turning it several times and making sure you roll it out enough—thick dough is harder to cook. Try whatever toppings you like to create your own masterpiece.

2 andouille sausages

2 portobella mushrooms

2 tablespoons (30 ml) vegetable oil, divided

All-purpose flour, for dusting

1 pound (454 g) premade or homemade pizza dough

1 cup (250 g) prepared pizza sauce

2 cups (230 g) shredded mozzarella cheese

4 large eggs

1. Grill the sausages until cooked through, turning often, about 6 minutes. Transfer the sausages to a plate and let cool enough to slice them.

2. Lightly brush the mushrooms with 1 tablespoon (15 ml) of oil and grill them until tender and lightly charred, turning once, about 5 minutes in total. You can grill the sausages and mushrooms at the same time. Transfer the mushrooms to a plate and slice thinly.

3. Lightly flour a large cutting board. On it, flatten and stretch the pizza dough with your hands until it is roughly 12 inches (30.5 cm) in diameter. Allow the dough to rest for 5 minutes.

4. Lightly oil the grill. Transfer the dough to the grill and grill until the bottom is lightly browned, lifting the edges to check, about 3 minutes. Rotate the dough and grill for 1 more minute.

5. Flip the dough over and, working quickly, spread the tomato sauce to the edges, top with the sausage, mushrooms, and cheese. Crack the eggs on the pizza, closer to the center so they don't drip off.

6. Continue to grill until the egg whites are set and the cheese is melted, rotating the pizza several times to prevent the bottom crust from getting too dark, about 4 to 6 minutes.

7. Slide the pizza onto the cutting board, slice, and serve.

Servings:
4 people

Prep time:
10 minutes

Cook time:
10 minutes

Cooking Accessory:
Cast-Iron Griddle Top

Sweet Potato Pancakes

If you like pumpkin pie, these golden, warmly spiced pancakes will delight you. If your griddle is a smidge too hot, you can flip the pancakes more frequently so they don't get too dark. These are delicious with a generous spoon of apple butter instead of traditional syrup.

¾ cup (94 g) all-purpose flour

1½ tablespoons (23 g) brown sugar

1 teaspoon baking powder

½ teaspoon ground cinnamon

¼ teaspoon ground nutmeg

Pinch sea salt

½ cup (120 ml) milk

½ cup (113 g) cooked mashed sweet potato

1 large egg

1 teaspoon canola oil, plus extra for greasing

Maple syrup, for serving

Fresh fruit of choice, for serving

1. In a large bowl, combine the flour, brown sugar, baking powder, cinnamon, nutmeg, and salt until well mixed.

2. In a small bowl, whisk the milk, sweet potato, egg, and 1 teaspoon of oil until smooth. Add the sweet potato mixture to the flour mixture and whisk until just moistened.

3. Lightly coat the griddle with vegetable oil. Scoop ¼ cup (60 ml) of batter per pancake onto the griddle and cook the pancakes until they have bubbles on the surface and the edges are firm, about 2 minutes. Flip them over and cook about 2 minutes more.

4. Serve two pancakes to each person warm with maple syrup and fresh fruit.

Servings:
4 people

Prep time:
10 minutes

Cook time:
10 minutes

Cooking Accessory:
Cast-Iron Griddle Top

Buttermilk Pancakes

Pancakes aren't just for breakfast; they can be enjoyed for any meal or eaten cold with nut butter for a snack. If you don't have buttermilk, mix 1²/₃ cups (400 ml) of milk with 1 tablespoon (15 ml) of vinegar and let the mixture sit for a few minutes to curdle. For the best results, make sure your griddle is between 350°F and 375°F (177°C and 191°C).

2 cups (250 g) all-purpose flour

2 tablespoons (26 g) sugar

1 tablespoon (13.8 g) baking powder

½ teaspoon sea salt

1¾ cups (410 ml) buttermilk

1 large egg

2 tablespoons (30 ml) canola oil, plus extra for greasing the griddle

1 teaspoon vanilla extract

Maple syrup, for serving

1. In a large bowl, sift together the flour, sugar, baking powder, and salt. Whisk in the milk, egg, 2 tablespoons (30 ml) of oil, and vanilla until the batter is combined.

2. Preheat the griddle to 350°F (177°C) and lightly grease with oil.

3. Scoop ¼ cup (60 ml) of batter per pancake onto the griddle and cook 4 pancakes at a time. Cook each pancake until its bottom is golden brown and the bubbles on the surface burst, about 2 to 3 minutes. Flip the pancakes and cook about 2 minutes longer until browned on both sides.

4. Repeat with the remaining batter and serve topped with maple syrup.

Servings:
4 people

Prep time:
15 minutes

Cook time:
16 minutes

Cooking Accessory:
Cast-Iron Griddle Top

Coconut French Toast

Golden egg- and coconut milk–soaked bread is a delectable weekend morning treat. The orange in the egg mixture adds sweetness, so this dish can be served plain or with a bit of butter. If you're working in batches, scrape the coconut bits off the griddle before cooking additional batches to prevent burning.

4 large eggs

¾ cup (177 ml) canned coconut milk

¼ cup (60 ml) orange juice

1 teaspoon coconut extract

2 cups (160 g) shredded unsweetened coconut

Vegetable oil for greasing

8 slices brioche or white bread, ½ inch (1.3 cm) thick

Maple syrup, for serving

1. In a medium bowl, whisk the eggs, coconut milk, orange juice, and coconut extract until blended. Spread out the shredded coconut on a large plate and set next to the egg mixture.

2. Lightly grease the griddle with vegetable oil.

3. Dip the bread slices in the egg mixture, shaking off the excess, and dredge them in the coconut so that both sides are coated.

4. Place the slices on the griddle and cook until golden brown on both sides, turning once, about 4 minutes in total.

5. Serve 2 pieces per person with maple syrup.

Fire Pit Breakfasts

Servings:
4 people

Prep time:
5 minutes

Cook time:
10 minutes

Cooking Accessory:
Cast-Iron Grill Top

Foil-Packet Banana French Toast

French toast can be made in a foil packet with very little mess or fuss! Banana is a lovely addition, and if you want a sublime variation, spread the bread with peanut butter, too. Just make sure the aluminum foil packet is several layers thick and leakproof or all your eggy liquid will run out.

Nonstick cooking spray

3 large eggs

1 cup (240 ml) milk

2 tablespoons (30 g) brown sugar

1 teaspoon vanilla extract

¾ teaspoon ground cinnamon

¼ teaspoon ground nutmeg

8 slices stale bread, quartered

2 small ripe bananas, sliced

Maple syrup, for serving

1. Place a piece of aluminum foil (about 12 x 18 inches or 30.5 x 45.8 cm) on a clean work surface and lay a second layer (12 x 18 inches or 30.5 x 45.8 cm) across the first one. Fold the edges of the foil up to create walls and spray with oil.

2. In a medium bowl, whisk the eggs, milk, brown sugar, vanilla, cinnamon, and nutmeg until well blended.

3. Arrange the bread pieces in the packet and top with the banana slices. Pour the egg mixture over the bread, tossing to coat all the pieces.

4. Fold together the edges of the foil to seal the packet and place it on the grill. Cook undisturbed until the bread is toasty and golden, turning the packet several times, about 10 minutes.

5. Carefully open the packet and serve with maple syrup.

Sizzling Sides and Snacks

2

Servings:
4 people

Prep time:
15 minutes

Cook time:
10 minutes

Cooking Accessory:
Cast-Iron Grill Top

Grilled Mexican Street Corn (Elote)

Elotes are a top food trend worldwide for good reason; they are utterly delicious! Grilling the corn enhances its sweetness and the husks protect the kernels from burning. The toppings in this recipe are traditional, but you can add your own twist with different cheeses, hot peppers, and even a bit of guacamole.

4 ears corn, husks on

1/3 cup (75 g) mayonnaise

2 tablespoons (30 g) sour cream

Juice of ½ lime

1 teaspoon smoked chili powder

1/3 cup (90 g) crumbled cotija cheese

¼ cup (4 g) finely chopped fresh cilantro

1. Peel the husks back, leaving them attached at the bottom. Remove the silk and pull the husks over the corn kernels.

2. Arrange the corn on the grill, and cook, turning often, until the corn is tender and lightly charred, about 10 minutes.

3. Transfer the ears to a plate, let them cool until you can handle them, and then strip the husks off.

4. In a small bowl, mix the mayonnaise, sour cream, lime juice, and chili powder.

5. Spread the mayonnaise mixture all over the corn and sprinkle the ears with the cheese and cilantro.

Servings:
4 people

Prep time:
15 minutes

Cook time:
8–10 minutes

Lacy Potato Pancakes

Potato pancakes are featured in many cuisines; who can resist shredded potato fried into a crispy, golden lattice? The trick to achieving a gorgeous texture is squeezing out as much water as possible from the potatoes. Try them with a scoop of sour cream or sautéed apples for a snack, or serve the pancakes as a special side dish when you have guests to impress.

3 large russet potatoes, scrubbed and grated

½ sweet onion, grated

3 tablespoons (21 g) breadcrumbs

1 large egg

1 tablespoon (8 g) cornstarch

Sea salt, to taste

Freshly ground black pepper, to taste

Canola oil, for greasing

1. Place the grated potato and onion in the center of a clean kitchen towel, gather the edges and pull inward to form a pouch, twist at the top, and squeeze out as much liquid as possible.

2. Transfer the potato and onion to a medium bowl and mix in the breadcrumbs, egg, and cornstarch. Season the mixture with salt and pepper to taste and let stand for 10 minutes.

3. Generously grease the griddle and scoop the mixture using a ¼-cup (60 ml) measuring cup. Flatten the potato mixture with a spatula and cook, turning halfway through, until golden brown and crispy, about 8 to 10 minutes in total.

4. Transfer the cooked pancakes to a paper towel–lined plate and blot the extra oil with an additional paper towel.

5. Serve.

Sizzling Sides and Snacks

Servings:
4 people

Prep time:
15 minutes

Cook time:
20 minutes

Loaded Baked Potatoes

Baked potatoes are a classic side dish, but also show up as fast food in some countries because they are inexpensive and the heaps of possible toppings suit any taste. This version uses sliced potatoes, which fry up quickly, rather than baked, but the taste is identical. You can swap in sweet potatoes for a different—yet equally delicious—dish.

8 slices bacon

4 medium russet potatoes, cut into ¼-inch (6-mm) slices

½ teaspoon paprika

Sea salt, to taste

Freshly ground black pepper, to taste

¾ cup (86 g) shredded mozzarella cheese

¾ cup (86 g) shredded cheddar cheese

1 scallion, white and green parts, thinly sliced

2 tablespoons (8 g) chopped fresh flat-leaf parsley

Sour cream, for serving

1. Cook the bacon on the griddle, turning once, until crispy, 5 to 6 minutes. Transfer the bacon to a cutting board and chop. Set aside.

2. While the bacon is cooking, toss the potato slices, paprika, salt, and pepper in a medium bowl.

3. After the bacon has been transferred to a plate, add the potatoes to the griddle and cook them in the bacon fat, tossing occasionally, until fork tender and golden, about 12 minutes.

4. Add the bacon bits and cheeses and cook, tossing, until the cheese is melted, about 2 minutes.

5. Serve the potatoes topped with scallions, parsley, and sour cream.

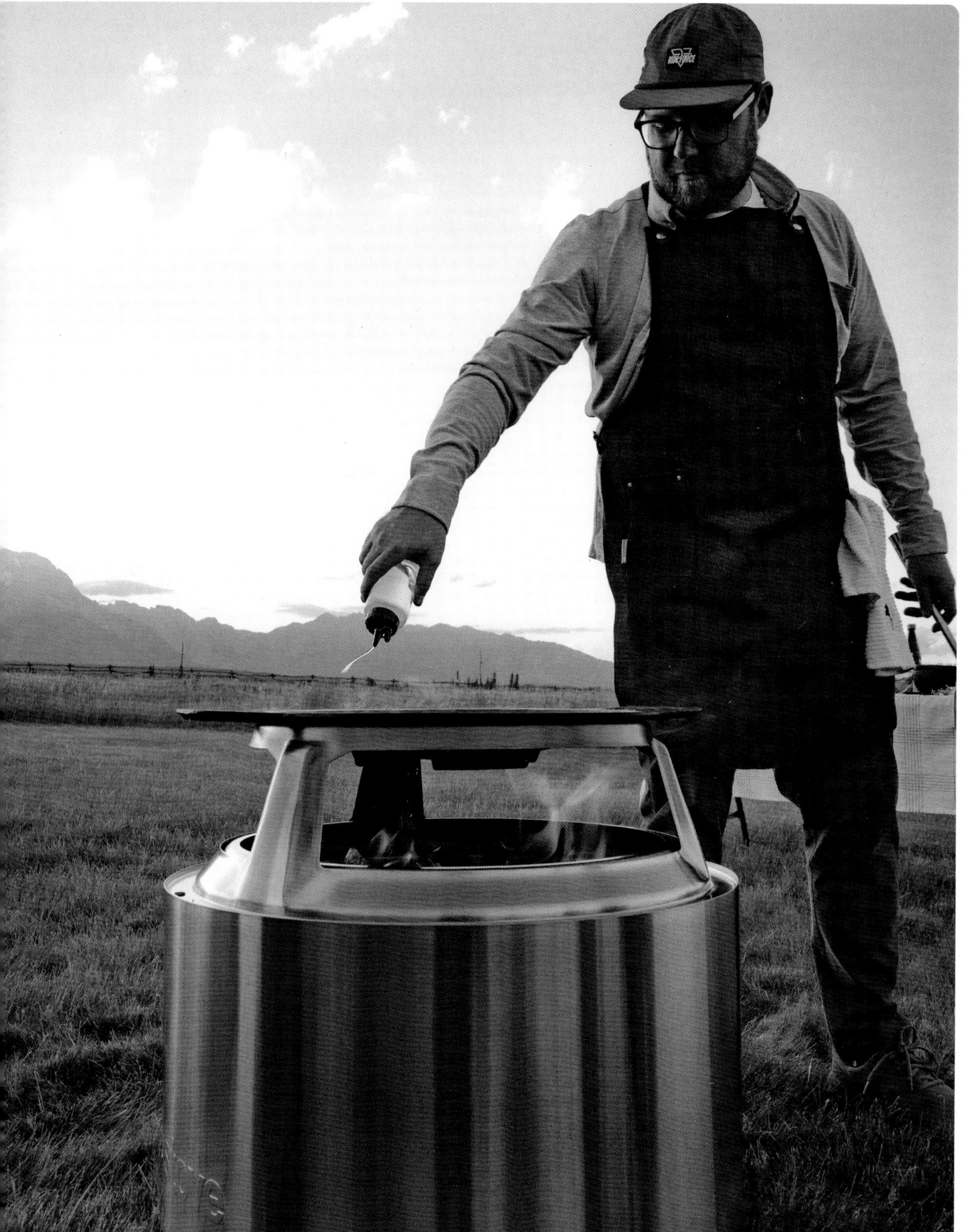

Servings:
4 people

Prep time:
15 minutes

Cook time:
6 minutes

Cooking Accessory:
Cast-Iron Griddle Top

Sun-dried Tomato Pesto Cauliflower Steaks

Who knew humble cauliflower could be a gourmet creation, packed with flavor and texture? Make sure you leave the base of the cauliflower head intact so your steaks don't fall apart when cooked. The edges—which will fall apart—can be used in another recipe. Regular pesto or marinara sauce is a fabulous substitution for the sun-dried pesto, if it is not available.

Nonstick cooking spray

1 head cauliflower, cut into 4 "steaks," about 1-inch (2.5-cm) wide

¼ cup (65 g) sun-dried tomato pesto

1 cup (100 g) shredded Parmesan cheese

¼ cup (75 g) marinated artichoke hearts, quartered

¼ cup (25 g) sliced kalamata olives

2 tablespoons (18 g) toasted pine nuts

1. Spray the griddle generously with oil and add the cauliflower steaks. Cook the steaks until lightly browned and tender-firm, turning once, about 4 minutes total.

2. Spread 1 tablespoon of pesto on each steak and sprinkle with Parmesan. Cook until the Parmesan is melted, about 2 minutes.

3. Serve the steaks topped with artichoke hearts, olives, and pine nuts.

Servings:
2 people

Prep time:
10 minutes

Cook time:
4 minutes

Cooking Accessory:
Cast-Iron Griddle Top

Monte Cristo Egg Melt

This simple sandwich has a rich, complex taste. Making it is messy fun; dipping the entire completed sandwich in the egg while holding it together isn't as hard as it sounds. Serve the sandwich with thick dill pickle spears or sliced tomatoes.

4 large eggs

Sea salt, to taste

Freshly ground black pepper, to taste

4 thick bread slices

2 tablespoons (22 g) Dijon mustard

8 slices smoked turkey or ham

4 slices Swiss cheese

Vegetable oil, for greasing

1. In a small bowl, whisk the eggs until well blended and season lightly with salt and pepper; set aside.

2. Place your bread on a clean work surface and spread the mustard evenly between the slices.

3. Top two slices with 4 pieces of turkey and two slices of cheese. Place the other two bread slices on top of the cheese to close the sandwiches.

4. Lightly oil the griddle.

5. Dredge the sandwiches in the egg mixture, shake off the excess, and transfer them to the griddle and cook until the bread is golden brown and the cheese is melted, about 2 minutes per side.

6. Serve immediately.

Servings:
4 people

Prep time:
15 minutes

Cook time:
6 minutes

Cooking Accessory:
Cast-Iron Griddle Top

Grilled Vegetable Open-Faced Sandwich

Imagine warm grilled vegetables heaped on lightly toasted crusty bread, accented with creamy goat cheese and sun-dried tomatoes. Tangy balsamic vinegar soaks into the bread along with the juices from the vegetables, creating an explosion of flavor in every bite. Sound delicious? Then read ahead to find out how you can make this delicious sandwich in less than 25 minutes. You can add grilled asparagus spears or French beans for a pretty variation.

½ small eggplant, sliced into ¼-inch-thick (6-mm-thick) rounds

1 zucchini, sliced into ½-inch-thick (1-cm-thick) rounds

½ red onion, thinly sliced

2 bell peppers, red and yellow, seeded and cut into ½-inch (1-cm) strips

3 tablespoons (45 ml) vegetable oil, divided

Sea salt, to taste

Freshly ground black pepper, to taste

4 (1-inch/2.5-cm-thick) slices crusty Italian or French bread

¼ cup (65 g) sun-dried tomato pesto

½ cup (75 g) crumbled goat cheese

1 tablespoon (15 ml) balsamic vinegar

1. In a large bowl, toss the eggplant, zucchini, onion, and bell peppers in 2 tablespoons (30 ml) of oil and season them lightly with salt and pepper.

2. Spread the vegetables on the griddle and sauté until lightly caramelized and tender, 4 to 5 minutes. Push the vegetables to the edge of the griddle.

3. Brush both sides of the bread with the remaining oil and place them on the griddle. Cook the bread, turning once, until it's golden, about 1 minute total.

4. Spread 1 tablespoon of sun-dried tomato pesto on each bread slice and top with the vegetables.

5. Divide the goat cheese between the sandwiches and drizzle them with balsamic vinegar.

6. Serve one open-faced sandwich per person.

Sizzling Sides and Snacks

Servings:
4 people

Prep time:
15 minutes

Cook time:
10 minutes

Cooking Accessory:
Cast-Iron Griddle Top

Blackened Salmon Po'Boy

The po'boy is a famous New Orleans sandwich, which was created as an inexpensive choice for unemployed striking streetcar drivers in 1929. This version features Cajun-spiced salmon topped with creamy yogurt and fresh vegetables. Chicken or shrimp makes a delicious filling if salmon isn't your first choice.

2 teaspoons (4 g) Cajun seasoning

4 (4-ounce/113-g) skinless salmon fillets

2 tablespoons (30 ml) vegetable oil

Juice of 1 lemon

4 crusty rolls, such as ciabatta rolls

¼ cup (60 g) plain Greek yogurt

2 small tomatoes, thinly sliced

2 cups (60 g) shredded spinach

2 scallions, white and green parts, sliced

1. Rub the Cajun seasoning all over the salmon fillets.

2. Drizzle the vegetable oil on the griddle and cook the salmon fillets on one side without turning for 4 minutes, until blackened, then flip the fillets over carefully and cook until the fish is cooked through, about 5 minutes.

3. Remove the salmon from the griddle and set aside on a plate. Drizzle with the lemon juice.

4. Split the rolls and toast them until golden, cut-side down, on the griddle for 1 minute.

5. Spread the inside of each bottom roll with the yogurt. Top the yogurt with the salmon fillets, tomatoes, spinach, and scallions, splitting the ingredients evenly between the four rolls.

6. Top with the top part of the roll and serve.

Servings:
4 people

Prep time:
15 minutes

Cook time:
22 minutes

Cooking Accessory:
Cast-Iron Grill Top

Grilled Chicken Flatbread Pizza

Naan bread makes perfect pizza without the fuss of handling dough. You can use any type of flatbread, such as focaccia or pita, with stellar results. The chicken and mushrooms can be cooked ahead and stored in the refrigerator until it is pizza-making time!

Nonstick cooking spray

2 (6-oz/170-g) boneless, skinless chicken breasts

Sea salt, to taste

Freshly ground black pepper, to taste

2 large portobella mushroom caps

½ cup (123 g) pizza sauce or basil pesto

4 large naan flatbreads

3 cups (345 g) shredded mozzarella cheese

1 cup (180 g) chopped roasted red peppers

Fresh basil, to taste

Crushed red pepper, to taste

1. Lightly spray the grill with nonstick cooking spray and season the chicken with salt and pepper. Grill the chicken breasts until cooked through, turning several times, 12 to 15 minutes total. About halfway through cooking, place the mushrooms on the grill and cook, turning often, until they are tender, about 6 minutes.

2. Transfer the chicken and mushrooms to a cutting board to chop.

3. Spread 2 tablespoons of sauce (or pesto) on each naan bread and top each with the cheese, chicken, mushrooms, and red peppers.

4. Grease the grill again and add the naan bread pizzas.

5. Grill until the cheese is melted and bubbly and the bread is lightly charred, about 7 minutes.

6. Top with fresh basil and crushed red pepper, then serve.

Cooking Accessory:
Cast-Iron Griddle or Grill Top

Servings:	Prep time:	Cook time:
4 people	15 minutes	10 minutes

Loaded Nachos

Cheesy nachos are ideal for sharing and are extra gooey when made in a handy foil packet. Don't skip spraying the foil with cooking spray or you won't be able to pry the chips off the bottom. You can toss the cooked meat with taco seasoning before adding it for an extra flavor boost.

Nonstick cooking spray

1 (10-oz/283 g) bag tortilla chips

2 cups (280 g) cooked ground beef or chicken

2 cups (520 g) store-bought salsa

1 (15-oz/425-g) can black beans, drained and rinsed

1 avocado, pitted, peeled, and cubed

2 cups (225 g) shredded Mexican cheese blend

2 scallions, white and green parts, thinly sliced

Chopped fresh cilantro, for garnishing

1. Lay an 18-by-12-inch (45-by-30-cm) piece of foil on your work surface. Lay a second piece (same size) across the first, overlapping in the middle.

2. Spray the foil with the nonstick cooking spray and spread one-third of the tortilla chips in the center. Top with one-quarter of the cooked meat, salsa, black beans, avocado, and cheese. Repeat for a second layer. For the last layer, use the remaining chips and meat, salsa, beans, and cheese.

3. Fold the edges of the foil over the nachos to create a sealed packet.

4. Place the packet on the grill or griddle and allow it to sit until the ingredients are heated through and the cheese is melted, about 10 minutes.

5. Serve topped with the scallions and cilantro.

Servings:
5 people

Prep time:
10 minutes

Cook time:
25 minutes

Cooking Accessory:
Cast-Iron Griddle or Grill Top

Campfire Sandwiches

Have you ever tried pull apart bread made in the oven? This is an elevated version that creates appetizing sandwiches perfect for late-night snacking or to combat afternoon munchies. Any type of filling works, including olives, sun-dried tomatoes, sliced onions, or even pickles.

1 loaf Italian or French bread

¼ cup (55 g) butter, softened

¼ cup (60 g) mayonnaise

2 tablespoons (22 g) stone-ground mustard

10 slices cheese (cheddar, Swiss, Gruyère, Havarti, Gouda)

15 slices assorted deli meats (chicken, roast beef, ham, pastrami, hot salami)

1. Cut 9 slits in the bread—top to bottom—leaving about ½ inch (1 cm) attached at the bottom.

2. In a small bowl, combine the butter, mayonnaise, and mustard and spread the mixture generously in the first cut, starting on one side, and then in every second cut.

3. Layer 1 slice of cheese, 3 pieces of deli meat, and a second slice of cheese into 5 stacks. Stuff each stack into the slits with the butter mixture, taking care to press each bundle to the bottom of each opening.

4. Wrap the entire loaf in a double layer of greased foil to create a sealed package.

5. Place the package on a grill or griddle and cook until heated through and the cheese is melted, turning several times, 20 to 25 minutes.

6. Open the foil packet and pull apart the sandwiches to serve.

3

Chapter 3
Sensational Skewers

Servings:	Prep time:	Cook time:
2 people	10 minutes plus 6 hours marinating	8 minutes

Cooking Accessory:
Cast-Iron Grill Top and
Roasting Sticks

Chili Shrimp

Sizzling shrimp on skewers seem like the perfect meal on a balmy summer evening in the company of friends or a special loved one. Honey and chili powder create the perfect sweet-to-heat balance, especially with the tang of lime. Make sure you leave the tails on the shrimp so you have something to hold while eating, and keep some napkins handy to mop up the juices.

Juice and zest of 1 lime

2 teaspoons (10 ml) extra-virgin olive oil

1 tablespoon (20 g) honey

½ teaspoon smoked paprika

¼ teaspoon chili powder

Freshly ground black pepper, to taste

12 jumbo (21/30 count) shrimp, peeled and deveined

Chopped fresh cilantro, for garnishing

1. In a medium bowl, whisk the lime juice, lime zest, olive oil, honey, paprika, chili powder, and black pepper. Add the shrimp and toss to combine.

2. Cover the bowl and refrigerate for at least 6 hours.

3. Thread 3 shrimp each on wooden skewers that have been soaked for 30 minutes in water. Discard any remaining marinade.

4. Arrange the shrimp on the grill and cook, turning every 2 minutes, until cooked through, 6 to 8 minutes.

5. Sprinkle with cilantro and serve 2 skewers per person.

Servings:
2 people

Prep time:
15 minutes
plus 30 minutes
soaking the
skewers

Cook time:
20 minutes

Grilled Chicken Wing Kebabs

Why make chicken wing skewers when you can just grill them individually? Because it's fun and quick! Any kind of sauce can be brushed on the wings—buffalo, honey garlic, teriyaki—or you can grill them with a simple salt and pepper finish. Serve these skewers with dipping sauce, like ranch or blue cheese.

12 chicken wings, flats and drumettes

Sea salt, to taste

Freshly ground black pepper, to taste

1 cup (240 g) ketchup

¼ cup (80 g) maple syrup

1 tablespoon (7.5 g) chipotle chili powder

2 teaspoons (6 g) garlic powder

1 teaspoon celery salt

1. Soak wooden skewers in water for 30 minutes.

2. Thread 3 wings onto each skewer, leaving a bit of space between them for even cooking.

3. Season the wings with salt and pepper.

4. In a small bowl, mix the ketchup, maple syrup, chili powder, garlic powder, and celery salt until well blended. Taste and adjust the seasoning.

5. Grill the skewers, turning occasionally, until the wings are cooked through and golden, about 20 minutes. Start basting the wings with the sauce at 10 minutes.

6. Serve.

Servings:
4 people

Prep time:
30 minutes
plus 1 hour
marinating

Cook time:
16 minutes

Cooking Accessory:
Cast-Iron Grill Top and
Roasting Sticks

Chicken Satay with Peanut Sauce

Satays are kebabs without the chunks of vegetables, and usually feature complex spice profiles. The peanut sauce in this recipe is a traditional accompaniment for Indonesian food, but you can substitute your favorite dipping sauce. Next time you have friends over for a fire, serve these flavorful skewers on a pretty platter and wait for the compliments.

For satays

1 pound (454 g) boneless, skinless chicken breast, cut into ½-inch (1-cm) strips

Juice of 1 lime

2 tablespoons (30 ml) olive oil

1½ tablespoons (23 g) brown sugar

2 teaspoons (6 g) minced garlic

For the sauce

½ cup (130 g) peanut butter

3 tablespoons (44 ml) low-sodium soy sauce

1 tablespoon (20 g) honey

1 teaspoon grated fresh ginger

Juice of 1 lime

¼ teaspoon red pepper flakes (optional)

1. In a large bowl, toss the chicken, lime juice, oil, brown sugar, and garlic to coat the chicken. Cover the bowl and refrigerate for at least 1 hour to marinate.

2. Meanwhile, in a small bowl, whisk together the peanut butter, soy sauce, honey, ginger, lime juice, and red pepper flakes (if using) until smooth. Add water by the tablespoon until you reach the desired consistency.

3. Remove the chicken from the marinade and thread each strip onto wooden skewers that have been soaked in water for 30 minutes.

4. Arrange the skewers on the grill and cook until cooked through and golden, about 4 minutes per side.

5. Serve with the dipping sauce.

Servings:
4 people

Prep time:
10 minutes
plus 2 hours
marinating

Cook time:
10 minutes

Cooking Accessory:
Cast-Iron Grill Top and
Roasting Sticks

Herbed Steak Skewers

Herbs and tangy balsamic vinegar add a lovely flavor to hearty steak chunks, a nice departure from classic barbecue sauce. Use a better cut of beef for these skewers because they will not be on the grill very long. You can add a few chunks of zucchini or onion to the skewers to round out the meal.

¼ cup (60 ml) extra-virgin olive oil

2 tablespoons (30 ml) balsamic vinegar

2 tablespoons (14 g) smoked paprika

1 tablespoon (2.7 g) dried thyme

1 tablespoon (3 g) dried oregano

1 tablespoon (10 g) minced garlic

1 tablespoon (1.3 g) dried parsley

2 teaspoons (5 g) ground cumin

1 pound (454 g) New York strip steaks, trimmed and cut into 1½-inch (3.8-cm) chunks

1. In a large bowl, whisk together the oil, vinegar, paprika, thyme, oregano, garlic, parsley, and cumin until well blended.

2. Add the steak, stirring to coat, cover, and refrigerate for at least 2 hours.

3. Thread the steak chunks onto 8 wooden skewers that have been soaked in water for 30 minutes.

4. Place the skewers on the grill and cook, turning occasionally, until the meat is browned on all sides and cooked to the desired doneness, 8 to 10 minutes for medium.

5. Serve.

Cooking Accessory:
Cast-Iron Grill Top and
Roasting Sticks

Servings:	Prep time:	Cook time:
4 people	20 minutes plus 30 minutes soaking the skewers	25 minutes

Gyros Meatball Kebab

Gyros consist of seasoned meat— pork, beef, chicken, or lamb— cooked on a vertical rotisserie and then thinly sliced and served wrapped in pita bread with various toppings. This version is close to the original in flavor and takes much less time on the Solo Stove. Serve these meatballs in the traditional way in pita or enjoy them with a creamy tzatziki sauce.

½ cup (60 g) seasoned breadcrumbs

1 pound (454 g) (80/20) ground beef

½ pound (227 g) ground pork

½ small sweet onion, minced

1 tablespoon (10 g) minced garlic

1 large egg

¼ cup (60 ml) milk

¼ cup (15 g) finely chopped flat-leaf parsley

2 teaspoons (2 g) dried oregano

Zest of 1 lemon

½ teaspoon sea salt

¼ teaspoon freshly ground black pepper

1. Soak 8 wooden skewers in water for 30 minutes.

2. In a large bowl, combine all of the ingredients using your hands, until very well combined.

3. Then, form the mixture into 1½-inch (3.8-cm) balls (about 1½ tablespoons each) and thread 4 meatballs onto each skewer. You should have 32 meatballs.

4. Arrange the skewers on the grill and cook the meatballs, turning several times, until they are golden and cooked through, 20 to 25 minutes in total.

5. Serve!

Servings:
4 people

Prep time:
10 minutes
plus 4 hours
marinating

Cook time:
12 minutes

Cooking Accessory:
Cast-Iron Grill Top and
Roasting Sticks

Maple Chili Chicken Kebabs

Maple syrup is the perfect ingredient for marinade because it caramelizes when grilled, creating a luscious finish on the chicken. Look for pure maple syrup because some products add fillers like corn syrup. This recipe would be delicious with shrimp or pork.

¼ cup (60 ml) soy sauce

¼ cup (80 g) maple syrup

½ teaspoon chili powder

2 (8-ounce/227-g) boneless, skinless chicken breasts, cut into 1-inch (2.5-cm) chunks

1 red bell pepper, cut into 1-inch (2.5-cm) chunks

1 red onion, cut into 1-inch (2.5-cm) chunks

1. Combine the soy sauce, maple syrup, and chili powder in a large resealable bag. Add the chicken chunks and massage until the chicken is well coated. Press the air out of the bag and seal it. Refrigerate the chicken for at least 4 hours, up to 12 hours.

2. Soak 8 wooden skewers in water for 30 minutes.

3. Thread the chicken pieces, red bell pepper, and onion onto the skewers, leaving a little space between the pieces.

4. Grill the chicken skewers until cooked through and lightly charred, turning several times, about 12 minutes in total.

5. Serve 2 skewers per person.

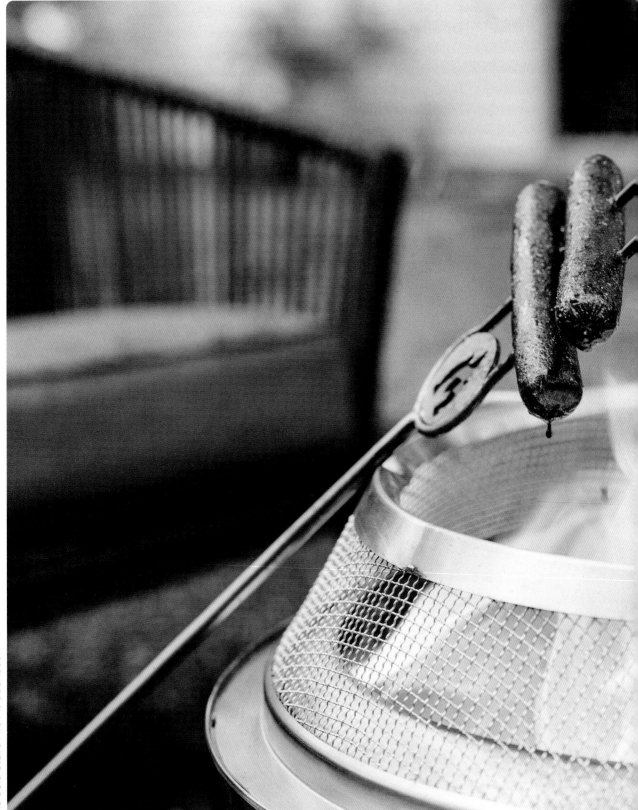

Servings:
4 people

Prep time:
15 minutes
plus 30 minutes
soaking the
skewers

Cook time:
12 minutes

Cooking Accessory:
Cast-Iron Grill Top and
Roasting Sticks

Cajun Salmon Skewers

Salmon is ideal for grilling because this fish is rich in healthy oils and has a robust texture. It holds together well on skewers and does not dry out. These skewers would be fabulous with a mixed green salad or a rice pilaf if you want a heartier meal.

1 pound (454 g) boneless, skinless salmon fillet, cut into 1½-inch (3.8-cm) cubes

2 teaspoons (4 g) Cajun seasoning

2 zucchini, cut into ½-inch (1.3-cm) chunks

1 small red onion, cut into 1-inch (2.5-cm) chunks

1 tablespoon (15 ml) vegetable oil

Sea salt, to taste

Freshly ground black pepper, to taste

1. Soak 8 wooden skewers in water for 30 minutes.

2. Place the salmon in a medium bowl and toss with the Cajun seasoning until the chunks are coated.

3. Place the zucchini, onion, and oil in a small bowl, season with salt and pepper, and toss to evenly coat.

4. Thread the salmon, zucchini, and onion onto the skewers, alternating the fish with the vegetables.

5. Arrange the salmon skewers on the grill and cook until the fish is opaque and the vegetables tender, turning halfway through, about 10 to 12 minutes in total.

6. Serve 2 skewers per person.

Servings:
4 people

Prep time:
15 minutes
plus 1 hour
marinating

Cook time:
15 minutes

Cooking Accessory:
Cast-Iron Grill Top and
Roasting Sticks

Tzatziki Chicken Skewers

Oregano and lemon take center stage in this Greek-inspired marinade. The accompanying tzatziki sauce is also a nod to the spectacular cuisine of Greece. You can make the sauce three to four days ahead and store it refrigerated in an airtight container until you are ready to serve this meal.

For the Skewers

¼ cup (60 ml) extra-virgin olive oil

Juice of 1 lemon

2 tablespoons (6 g) dried oregano

1 teaspoon garlic powder

½ teaspoon sea salt

¼ teaspoon freshly ground black pepper

4 (5-oz/425 g) boneless, skinless chicken breasts or thighs, cut into 1-inch (2.5-cm) chunks

For the Tzatziki Sauce

¾ cup (184 g) plain Greek yogurt

½ English cucumber, grated, liquid squeezed out

1 tablespoon (6 g) chopped fresh mint

1 teaspoon minced garlic

Sea salt, to taste

1. In a large resealable plastic bag, combine the oil, lemon juice, oregano, garlic powder, salt, and pepper. Add the chicken chunks, press the air out, seal, and refrigerate for at least 1 hour, up to 8 hours.

2. While the chicken is marinating, make the tzatziki sauce. In a small bowl, combine the yogurt, cucumber, mint, garlic, and salt. Cover the sauce and refrigerate until you are serving the skewers.

3. Soak 8 wooden skewers in water for 30 minutes.

4. Thread the chicken onto the skewers and discard the marinade.

5. Arrange the skewers on the grill and cook, turning several times, until the chicken is cooked through, 12 to 15 minutes in total.

6. Serve with the tzatziki sauce.

Sensational Skewers

Servings:
4 people

Prep time:
10 minutes
plus 1 hour
marinating

Cook time:
15 minutes

Cooking Accessory:
Cast-Iron Grill Top and
Roasting Sticks

Hawaiian-Inspired Pork Kebabs

Ginger- and lime-accented pork pieces combined with sweet pineapple and piquant red onion are a wonderful main course when friends and family gather for a meal. Watch the skewers carefully on the grill because the addition of brown sugar in the marinade means caramelization happens quickly.

½ cup (118 ml) extra-virgin olive oil

Juice of 2 limes

¼ cup (4 g) chopped fresh cilantro

2 tablespoons (30 g) brown sugar

2 teaspoons (4 g) minced ginger

1 teaspoon (3 g) minced garlic

½ teaspoon sea salt

1 pound (454 g) center-cut pork chops, cut into 1-inch (2.5-cm) chunks

1 red onion, cut into 1-inch (2.5-cm) chunks

16 pineapple chunks, fresh or canned

1. In a large resealable plastic bag, combine the oil, lime juice, cilantro, brown sugar, ginger, garlic, and salt. Add the pork chunks, press the air out, seal, and refrigerate for at least 1 hour, up to 8 hours.

2. Soak 8 wooden skewers in water for 30 minutes.

3. Thread the pork, onion, and pineapple onto the skewers and discard the remaining marinade.

4. Arrange the skewers on the grill and cook, turning several times, until the pork is cooked and lightly charred, about 15 minutes in total.

Servings:
4 people

Prep time:
15 minutes
plus 30 minutes
soaking the
skewers

Cook time:
6–8 minutes

Cooking Accessory:
Cast-Iron Grill Top and
Roasting Sticks

Buffalo Cauliflower Kebabs

Nutritional yeast might be an unfamiliar ingredient for you, but don't exclude it, if possible. It adds a delightful cheesy taste to this classic buffalo sauce. To ensure the best results, cut the florets with enough stalk to hold the pieces together when skewered and grilled.

¾ cup (177 ml) melted butter

¾ cup (177 ml) hot sauce (like Frank's)

¼ cup (15 g) nutritional yeast

1 large head cauliflower, cut into florets

Sea salt, to taste

Freshly ground black pepper, to taste

Blue cheese dressing, for serving

1. Soak 8 to 12 wooden skewers in water for 30 minutes.

2. Meanwhile, in a large bowl, whisk the butter, hot sauce, and nutritional yeast until combined. Add the cauliflower, season with salt and pepper, and toss to coat.

3. Thread the cauliflower florets onto the skewers, and reserve the sauce left in the bowl.

4. Arrange the kebabs on the grill and cook for 2 or 3 minutes, turn, and brush the skewers with the reserved sauce. Grill for 4 or 5 minutes longer, until the florets are lightly charred and tender.

5. Serve with blue cheese dressing.

4

Chapter 4
Main Courses

Servings:
3 people

Prep time:
5 minutes

Cook time:
10 minutes

Cooking Accessory:
Cast-Iron Griddle Top

Classic Egg Foo Young

This is not traditional egg foo young, but the method and basic ingredients are inspired by the Chinese dish Fu Yung Egg Slices. Take this variation and add your own spin with cooked chicken, shrimp, pepperoni, or ham if you want a more substantial meal. Make sure the griddle is between 300°F and 325°F (149°C and 163°C) for the best results.

8 large eggs

Sea salt, to taste

Freshly ground black pepper, to taste

1 tablespoon (15 ml) sesame oil, divided

1 cup (70 g) sliced mushrooms

1 tablespoon (6 g) grated fresh ginger

1 teaspoon minced garlic

6 cups (750 g) mung bean sprouts

1 red bell pepper, seeded and diced finely

1 scallion, white and green parts, chopped

1. In a medium bowl, whisk the eggs until well combined and season lightly with salt and pepper. Set the bowl aside.

2. Heat 2 teaspoons (10 ml) of oil on the griddle and add the mushrooms, ginger, and garlic. Sauté about 1 minute until fragrant.

3. Add the bean sprouts and red pepper and sauté until the vegetables are softened, about 4 minutes.

4. Divide the vegetables on the griddle into 4 equal mounds, spreading them out into rough circles.

5. Season with pepper and stir to combine well.

6. Wipe out the griddle with paper towels and add the remaining oil.

7. Pour about one-quarter of the egg mixture on each vegetable mound and cook until the eggs are lightly browned and cooked through, flipping once, about 4 minutes in total.

8. Transfer the omelets to a plate, stacking them on top of each other.

9. Serve immediately topped with chopped scallion.

Main Courses

Servings:
2 people

Prep time:
15 minutes

Cook time:
14 minutes

Cheesy Grilled Eggplant Stacks

Eggplant is spectacular when grilled, and meaty enough to be the base of a filling meal. Cooking the stack components separately ensures the goat cheese melts into a delicious gooey texture. If you want a more intense tomato flavor, substitute sun-dried tomatoes for fresh tomatoes.

1 large eggplant, ends trimmed off and cut lengthwise into 8 equal slices

½ teaspoon sea salt

2 tablespoons (30 ml) vegetable oil

Freshly ground black pepper, to taste

1 (10.5-oz/300 g) log goat cheese, cut into 8 slices

2 large tomatoes, ends trimmed off and cut into 8 slices

Chopped fresh basil, for garnishing

Balsamic vinegar, for drizzling

1. Sprinkle the eggplant with salt on both sides and set aside for 10 minutes. Blot the eggplant with a paper towel and brush both sides with oil. Season with pepper.

2. Grill the eggplant, turning once, until it is lightly charred and tender, about 12 minutes.

3. Top the eggplant with the goat cheese and a tomato slice and continue grilling until the cheese softens, about 2 minutes.

4. Transfer to two plates, making two towers on each plate by doubling up the stacks of eggplant, cheese, and tomato.

5. Garnish with basil and a drizzle of balsamic vinegar.

Servings:
4 people

Prep time:
30 minutes

Cook time:
15 minutes

Cooking Accessory:
Cast-Iron Wok Top

Teriyaki Vegetable Stir-Fry

Stir-fry meals are a no-brainer in the Solo Stove Wok, which makes cooking simple, quick, and flavorful. Try all your favorite veggies in this dish, such as baby corn, scallions, different mushrooms, bamboo shoots, French beans, or mung bean sprouts. If you don't have the wok accessory, the griddle will work as well.

For the Teriyaki Sauce

½ cup (118 ml) low-sodium soy sauce

2 tablespoons (40 g) honey

1 tablespoon (6 g) minced fresh ginger

2 teaspoons (6 g) minced garlic

For the Vegetable Stir-Fry

1 tablespoon (15 ml) sesame oil

1 cup (70 g) sliced shiitake mushrooms

1 large carrot, thinly sliced

2 large red bell peppers, seeded and thinly sliced

1 small broccoli head, cut into small florets

4 baby bok choy, washed and quartered

1 cup (64 g) snow peas

½ cup (73 g) chopped peanuts

1. In a small bowl, combine the soy sauce, honey, ginger, and garlic. Set aside.

2. Heat the oil in the wok and sauté the mushrooms until tender and lightly browned, about 8 minutes.

3. Add the carrots, red pepper, broccoli, and bok choy to the mushrooms and stir-fry until the vegetables are bright in color and tender, about 6 minutes.

4. Add the snow peas and teriyaki sauce and toss, until the sauce is heated through, about 1 minute.

5. Serve topped with chopped peanuts.

Main Courses

Servings:
4 people

Prep time:
10 minutes

Cook time:
10 minutes

Cooking Accessory:
Cast-Iron Griddle Top

Salmon Patties

Tamari sauce, ginger, and honey add an Asian flair to these patties, which you can play up with a hoisin slaw topping if you serve these with a bun. Try to pick up wild salmon whenever possible because its natural red color and firm, meaty texture create picture-perfect burgers.

3 tablespoons (45 ml) low-sodium tamari sauce

1 tablespoon (20 g) honey

1 pound (454 g) skinless salmon fillet, chopped into ¼-inch (6-mm) pieces

1 large egg, lightly beaten

1 scallion, white and green parts, finely chopped

1 tablespoon (8 g) grated fresh ginger

Vegetable oil

1. In a small bowl, stir together the tamari and honey and set it aside.

2. In a medium bowl, mix the salmon, egg, scallion, and ginger. Form the salmon mixture into 4 patties about 1-inch (2.5-cm) thick.

3. Coat the griddle lightly with oil. Cook the salmon burgers until cooked through, turning once, about 4 minutes per side. Brush the tamari-honey glaze over the patties and cook for 1 more minute per side, brushing more glaze after turning.

4. Serve plain or on a bun with your favorite toppings.

Servings:
4 people

Prep time:
15 minutes
plus 2 hours
marinating

Cook time:
5 minutes

Cooking Accessory:
Cast-Iron Grill Top

Grilled Calamari

Calamari might seem like a luxury ingredient, but it is often surprisingly inexpensive and easy to prepare. If you don't want to clean the squid yourself, look for a ready-to-cook option in the frozen section. Watch the calamari carefully when grilling; it cooks very quickly and too much time over the heat makes it rubbery.

1 teaspoon chili powder

½ teaspoon smoked paprika

½ teaspoon ground cumin

½ teaspoon ground coriander

2 teaspoons (10 ml) olive oil

3 large squid, cleaned, and split open with tentacles cut into rings

Sea salt, to taste

Freshly ground black pepper, to taste

Juice and zest of 1 lime

¼ cup (4 g) chopped cilantro

1. In a medium bowl, combine the chili powder, paprika, cumin, coriander, and olive oil until a paste forms. Add the squid to the bowl and rub the spice paste all over it using your hands. Cover the bowl and marinate in the refrigerator for at least 2 hours.

2. Arrange the calamari on the grill and cook until it is tender and lightly charred, turning once, about 5 minutes total. Season with salt and pepper.

3. Drizzle the calamari with lime juice and serve topped with cilantro and lime zest.

Servings:
4 people

Prep time:
15 minutes plus
chilling time

Cook time:
12 minutes

Seared Halibut with Citrus Compound Butter

Compound butter is a stellar method to add intense, rich flavor to any meal. It can be made ahead and frozen for up to three months; you just cut off the amount you need and pop the roll back in the freezer. Try it on any protein or veggies.

½ cup (115 g) butter, softened

Zest and juice of 1 lemon

2 teaspoons (6 g) minced garlic

1 shallot, minced

1 tablespoon (4 g) chopped fresh flat-leaf parsley

4 (5-oz/142-g) halibut fillets, about 1-inch (2.5-cm) thick

Sea salt, to taste

Freshly ground black pepper, to taste

2 tablespoons (30 ml) vegetable oil

1. In a small bowl, mix the butter, lemon zest, lemon juice, garlic, shallot, and parsley until very well combined.

2. Transfer the butter mixture to a piece of plastic wrap and form it into a log. Roll the log in the plastic wrap and twist the ends. Place the log in the refrigerator and chill until firm.

3. Pat the fish dry with paper towels and then lightly season it with salt and pepper.

4. Heat the oil on the griddle and pan sear the fish until it is lightly browned and just cooked through, turning the fillets over once, about 12 minutes in total.

5. Cut 4 slices of butter ½-inch (1.3-cm) thick and place them on the warm fish to melt.

6. Serve.

Servings:
4 people

Prep time:
30 minutes

Cook time:
10 minutes

Cooking Accessory:
Cast-Iron Griddle Top

Fish Tacos

The simple ingredients in fish tacos come together as a well-balanced meal, in both texture and taste. Any firm fish will work, such as halibut, grouper, red snapper, or salmon, if you enjoy its more assertive flavor. For a nice touch, wrap the corn tortillas in a clean kitchen cloth and set them on the griddle handle to warm.

¼ cup (31 g) all-purpose flour

¼ cup (35 g) cornmeal

½ teaspoon chili powder

⅛ teaspoon sea salt

⅛ teaspoon freshly ground black pepper

4 (6-oz/170-g) haddock fillets, cut into 8 strips

¼ cup (60ml) vegetable oil

8 small corn tortillas

Juice of 1 lime

1 small avocado, peeled, pitted, and diced

1 tomato, diced

¼ small red onion, thinly sliced

1 cup (43 g) shredded lettuce

1. In a small bowl, whisk the flour, cornmeal, chili powder, salt, and pepper.

2. Dredge the fish in the flour mixture until coated.

3. Heat the oil on the griddle and cook the fish until it is golden and flakes with a fork, turning halfway through, about 10 minutes in total.

4. Transfer the fish to a paper towel–lined plate.

5. Place a fish piece in each tortilla and squeeze lime juice over each one. Top each taco with avocado, tomato, onion, and lettuce and serve 2 tacos per person.

Servings:
4 people

Prep time:
15 minutes

Cook time:
30 minutes

Cooking Accessory:
Cast-Iron Griddle Top

Classic Shore Lunch

There is nothing like freshly caught fish battered and cooked up in a cast-iron skillet over a crackling campfire with heaps of golden fried potatoes and onions on the side. You can duplicate that experience with this recipe in your backyard or cottage. Most grocery stores carry rainbow trout, so pick some up cleaned and deboned for a delicious feast.

4 (5-oz/142-g) rainbow trout fillets

Sea salt, to taste

Freshly ground black pepper, to taste

¼ cup (60 ml) vegetable oil, divided

1 pound (454 g) fingerling potatoes, halved lengthwise

1 small sweet onion, halved and thinly sliced

1 teaspoon paprika

1 tablespoon (4 g) finely chopped fresh dill

Lemon wedges, for serving

1. Pat the fish dry with paper towels and season it with salt and pepper. Set the fish aside.

2. Heat 3 tablespoons (45 ml) of oil on the griddle and add the potatoes and onions. Season with paprika, salt, and pepper and sauté until the potatoes are golden and crispy and the onions tender, 18 to 20 minutes.

3. Push the potatoes and onions to the edge of the griddle and add the remaining oil to the center.

4. Pan-fry the fish, skin-side down, until the fish is flaky and the skin crispy, 10 minutes.

5. Serve the fish with a generous scoop of potatoes and onions, garnished with dill and lemon wedges.

Servings:
4 people

Prep time:
20 minutes

Cook time:
15 minutes

Cooking Accessory:
Cast-Iron Griddle Top

Chicken Fajitas

Who doesn't enjoy the spectacle of sizzling, smoking fajitas making their way to the table in a restaurant? Plus, it is fun to put them together with all the various toppings. The cast-iron griddle is ideal for creating a large quantity of chicken, peppers, and onions, so double up the recipe when you have a crowd to feed.

For the Fajitas

1 teaspoon ground cumin

½ teaspoon garlic powder

½ teaspoon chipotle chili powder

½ teaspoon smoked paprika

¼ teaspoon onion powder

⅛ teaspoon cayenne pepper

1 pound (454 g) boneless, skinless chicken breast, cut into ¼-inch (6-mm) strips

2 tablespoons (30 ml) vegetable oil, divided

2 red bell peppers, seeded and thinly sliced

1 green bell pepper, seeded and thinly sliced

1 small sweet onion, halved and thinly sliced

8 (6-inch/15-cm) tortillas

Toppings

Prepared or homemade salsa

Sour cream

Pickled jalapeños

Shredded lettuce

1. In a medium bowl, mix the cumin, garlic powder, chili powder, paprika, onion powder, and cayenne until well combined. Reserve 1 teaspoon of the spice mixture and set it aside.

2. Add the chicken to the bowl and toss to coat.

3. Heat 1 tablespoon (15 ml) of oil on half the griddle and sauté the chicken on the oiled surface until it is cooked through, about 15 minutes.

4. Halfway through the cooking time, heat the remaining oil on the other half of the griddle and sauté the peppers and onions until tender and lightly browned, seasoning them with the reserved spice mix.

5. Serve the chicken and vegetables tucked into the tortillas with your favorite toppings.

Main Courses

Servings:
4 people

Prep time:
5 minutes

Cook time:
16 minutes

Cooking Accessory:
Cast-Iron Grill Top

Simply Good Paprika Chicken

There is a famous Hungarian chicken dish—Paprikash—that features tender poultry in a tempting paprika and sour cream sauce. This recipe is inspired by those flavors, but takes a fraction of the time on a grill instead of braising in the oven. Try it with a dollop of sour cream if you like traditional combinations.

Vegetable oil, for greasing

4 (4-oz/113-g) boneless, skinless chicken breasts

1 teaspoon paprika

1 teaspoon ground cumin

¼ teaspoon ground coriander

Sea salt, to taste

Freshly ground black pepper, to taste

Sour cream, for serving

Green onions, sliced, for garnish

1. Lightly oil the grill.

2. Season the chicken breasts evenly with the paprika, cumin, coriander, salt, and pepper.

3. Arrange the chicken breasts on the grill and cook until they are golden brown and cooked through, 7 to 8 minutes per side.

4. Remove the breasts from the heat and let them stand for 5 minutes before slicing each breast into 3 pieces.

5. Place the chicken on a plate. Spoon dollops of sour cream onto the plate, top with sliced green onions, and serve.

The Solo Stove Fire Pit Cookbook

Servings:
4 people

Prep time:
15 minutes

Cook time:
19 minutes

Cooking Accessory:
Cast-Iron Wok Top

Chicken "Chow Mein"

Chow mein is an American-Chinese invention that usually combines various vegetables (often things like bean sprouts and water chestnuts) with meat and is typically served over fried noodles. Our version leans into the bean sprouts and leaves out the fried noodles, for a quicker and lower-carb main course. Double up the recipe for tasty leftovers for lunch; you will find this recipe delicious cold or hot.

1 cup (237 ml) vegetable stock

3 tablespoons (45 ml) low-sodium tamari sauce

2 tablespoons (16 g) cornstarch

1 tablespoon (20 g) honey

1 teaspoon (2.7 g) grated fresh ginger

Pinch red pepper flakes (optional)

1 tablespoon (15 ml) sesame oil, divided

½ pound (227 g) boneless, skinless chicken breast, cut into 1-inch (2.5-cm) chunks

1 cup (70 g) sliced button mushrooms

2 stalks celery, sliced

1 carrot, sliced into thin disks

1 red bell pepper, seeded and julienned

½ cup (33 g) snow peas, trimmed

2 cups (250 g) mung bean sprouts, washed thoroughly

2 scallions, white and green parts, thinly sliced

1 tablespoon (8 g) sesame seeds

1. In a small bowl, whisk the stock, tamari sauce, cornstarch, honey, ginger, and red pepper flakes (if using) together until well blended. Set aside.

2. Heat ½ tablespoon sesame oil in the wok. Sauté the chicken until it is cooked through, about 10 minutes. Transfer the chicken to a plate using a slotted spoon and set aside.

3. Heat the remaining oil in the wok and stir-fry the mushrooms, celery, carrot, and bell pepper until the vegetables are crisp-tender, about 4 minutes. Add the snow peas and bean sprouts and stir-fry for an additional 3 minutes.

4. Move the vegetables to the side of the wok and pour in the sauce. Whisk until the sauce is thick and glossy, about 2 minutes. Add the chicken back to the wok and toss with the sauce and vegetables.

5. Serve topped with the scallions and sesame seeds.

Main Courses

Servings:
4 people

Prep time:
10 minutes

Cook time:
10 minutes

Cooking Accessory:
Cast-Iron Grill Top

Really Juicy Hamburgers

Burgers are a natural meal to make over a campfire. Who can resist digging into a fully loaded patty on a toasted bun? These burgers are a mix of beef and pork for flavor but will work if your preference is 100 percent beef. Some of the toppings like bacon, sautéed mushrooms, and fried eggs can be made ahead on a griddle or in a cast-iron skillet placed on the grill.

1 pound (454 g) lean ground beef

½ pound (227 g) lean ground pork

1 large egg

½ small sweet onion, finely chopped

1 teaspoon minced garlic

¼ teaspoon sea salt

4 hamburger buns

Toppings

Lettuce

Cheese

Bacon

Mushrooms

Fried eggs

Pickles

Hot peppers

Condiments

1. In a medium bowl, mix the ground beef, ground pork, egg, onion, garlic, and salt until well combined.

2. Divide the meat mixture into 4 equal pieces and form them into ½-inch-thick (1-cm-thick) patties.

3. Grill the burgers for 4 to 5 minutes per side, or until they reach the desired doneness.

4. Serve on the buns with your favorite toppings.

Servings:
4 people

Prep time:
15 minutes

Cook time:
11 minutes

Vegetable Fried Rice

Fried rice is often served as a side dish, but it's a nice main course, as well. The best rice is a thoroughly chilled leftover, jasmine or basmati rice. Make sure you don't overmix the eggs when scrambling them because larger curds create a lovely texture.

4 large eggs

2 teaspoons (10 ml) low-sodium soy sauce

1 tablespoon (15 ml) sesame oil

2 stalks celery, finely diced

1 red bell pepper, seeded and finely diced

1 small carrot, peeled and finely diced

1 scallion, white and green parts, sliced on a bias

1 teaspoon minced garlic

1 teaspoon fresh grated ginger

3 cups (495 g) cooked white rice

1 cup (130 g) frozen peas

1. In a small bowl, whisk together the eggs and soy sauce and set aside.

2. Heat the oil in the wok.

3. Sauté the celery, red pepper, carrot, scallion, garlic, and ginger until the vegetables are softened, about 3 minutes.

4. Add the rice and sauté until well mixed and starting to brown, about 4 minutes.

5. Make a well in the center of the rice mixture down to the wok, exposing the surface.

6. Pour the egg mixture into the well in the rice and cook, stirring occasionally, until the egg is completely cooked through, about 3 minutes.

7. Add the frozen peas and sauté until warmed through, about 1 minute.

8. Serve.

Main Courses

Servings:
4 people

Prep time:
20 minutes

Cook time:
25 minutes

Cooking Accessory:
Cast-Iron Wok Top

Bahmi Goreng

The flavorings in bahmi are complex—hot, sweet, and salty. If you are not a fan of heat, reduce the amount of sambal oelek or omit it entirely.

½ cup (120 ml) chicken broth

¼ cup (60 ml) low-sodium soy sauce

2 tablespoons (30 g) brown sugar

2 tablespoons (30 g) sambal oelek or hot chili paste

2 tablespoons (30 ml) vegetable oil

1 pound (454 g) center-cut pork chops, cut into ½-inch (1.3-cm) chunks

2 leeks, white and green parts, halved lengthwise, thinly sliced, and washed thoroughly

1 sweet onion, halved and thinly sliced

2 teaspoons (6 g) minced garlic

2 teaspoons (5.4 g) grated fresh ginger

½ small green cabbage, finely shredded

2 medium carrots, shredded

5 cups (700 g) cooked egg noodles

Green onions, sliced, for garnish

1. In a small bowl, whisk the broth, soy sauce, brown sugar, and sambal oelek until blended. Set aside.

2. Heat the oil in the wok. Sauté the pork until it is cooked through, about 7 minutes. Transfer the pork using a slotted spoon to a plate and set it aside.

3. Sauté the leeks, onion, garlic, and ginger until softened, about 5 minutes. Add the cabbage and carrots and sauté until the vegetables are tender, about 10 minutes. Add the pork and any juices accumulated on the plate back to the wok.

4. Stir in the sauce, tossing to coat, and sauté until the liquid is reduced by half, about 2 minutes. Add the noodles and toss until they are heated through and well mixed with the other ingredients, 1 to 2 minutes.

5. Garnish with sliced green onions and serve.

Main Courses

Servings:
4 people

Prep time:
10 minutes

Cook time:
22 minutes

Cooking Accessory:
Cast-Iron Wok Top

Oktoberfest Bowl

There is a small city in Ontario, Canada, called Kitchener. Previously, it was called Berlin. The city's German heritage came from the Mennonites who originally settled there from Pennsylvania. This recipe is inspired by that city. Local pork, tender cabbage, and crisp apple tossed in a sweet, tart sauce spiked with hot mustard is a love song to this city's unique heritage.

½ cup (120 ml) low-sodium chicken broth

3 tablespoons (46 g) apple cider vinegar

2 tablespoons (30 g) brown sugar

1 tablespoon (11 g) Dijon mustard

1 tablespoon (8 g) cornstarch

¼ teaspoon caraway seeds (optional)

2 tablespoons (30 ml) vegetable oil, divided

4 (4-oz/113-g) boneless center-cut pork chops

Sea salt, to taste

Freshly ground black pepper, to taste

½ sweet onion, thinly sliced

1 teaspoon minced garlic

3 cups (210 g) finely shredded green cabbage

1 red apple, cored and chopped

1 tablespoon (4 g) chopped fresh flat-leaf parsley

(Recipe instructions on page 116)

(continued from page 114)

1. In a small bowl, whisk the chicken broth, apple cider vinegar, brown sugar, mustard, cornstarch, and caraway seeds (if using). Set aside.

2. Heat 1 tablespoon (15 ml) of oil in the wok. Lightly season the pork chops with salt and pepper and place them in the wok. Cook the pork until it has a golden crust and is just cooked through, turning several times, 10 to 12 minutes. Transfer the pork to a plate and cover it loosely with aluminum foil to keep it warm.

3. Add the remaining oil to the wok and sauté the onion and garlic until softened, about 3 minutes. Add the cabbage and apple and sauté, stirring, until crisp-tender, 4 to 5 minutes.

4. Move the vegetables to the side of the wok to create a clear cooking surface. Quickly re-stir the mustard sauce that was set aside earlier and add it to the cleared section. Cook, stirring often, until the sauce is thickened and hot, about 2 minutes. Toss the vegetables with the sauce and return the pork and any accumulated juices on the plate to the wok, turning to coat the meat in the sauce.

5. Serve topped with parsley.

Cooking Accessory:
Cast-Iron Grill Top

Servings:
4 people

Prep time:
5 minutes
plus 1 hour
marinating

Cook time:
20 minutes

Grilled Honey Mustard Chicken

Honey mustard sauce is a fan favorite for chicken wings, so why not try it with crispy grilled breasts? Butterflying chicken reduces cooking time and this marinade is high in sugar, so to prevent burning keep an eye on your chicken while it cooks. Thighs or drumsticks can be used instead of breast; just adjust the cooking time (less for drumsticks, more for thighs).

½ cup (88 g) Dijon mustard

⅓ cup (115 g) honey

Juice of 1 lemon

2 teaspoons (6 g) minced garlic

2 teaspoons (1.6 g) chopped fresh thyme

2 teaspoons (2.6 g) chopped fresh oregano

4 (5-oz/142-g) boneless chicken breasts, butterflied

Sea salt, to taste

Freshly ground black pepper, to taste

1. Combine the mustard, honey, lemon juice, garlic, thyme, and oregano in a large resealable plastic bag. Add the chicken breasts, squeeze out as much air as possible, seal, and refrigerate for at least 1 hour, up to 4 hours.

2. Grill the chicken until cooked through, turning several times, about 20 minutes in total.

3. Season with salt and pepper and serve.

Main Courses

Servings:	Prep time:	Cook time:
4 people	15 minutes plus 6 hours marinating	30 minutes

Cooking Accessory:
Cast-Iron Grill Top

Jerked Pork Tenderloin with Mango Salsa

Jerk seasoning is a blend of spices and herbs that create a sweet, savory, and spicy coating on meats and chicken. It originated in Jamaica, where all the ingredients could be grown and harvested. Make sure you marinate the meat for at least six hours to get the full flavor profile.

For the Mango Salsa

1 ripe mango, peeled, pitted, and diced

½ English cucumber, finely chopped

1 yellow bell pepper, finely chopped

½ red bell pepper, finely chopped

1 scallion, white and green parts, finely chopped

1 tablespoon (1 g) chopped fresh cilantro

Sea salt, to taste

For the Jerked Pork

2 tablespoons (30 ml) red wine vinegar

1 tablespoon (15 ml) olive oil

1 tablespoon (15 g) brown sugar

1 tablespoon (15 ml) freshly squeezed lime juice

2 teaspoons (10 ml) low-sodium soy sauce

1 teaspoon minced garlic

½ teaspoon ground allspice

½ teaspoon smoked chili powder

½ teaspoon thyme

¼ teaspoon ground cinnamon

Dash of ground cayenne pepper

Freshly ground black pepper, to taste

2 (10-oz/283 g) pork tenderloins, trimmed

1. In a small bowl, combine the mango, cucumber, bell peppers, scallion, and cilantro. Season with salt, cover, and refrigerate until you need it, up to 5 days.

2. In a medium bowl, whisk the red wine vinegar, oil, brown sugar, lime juice, soy sauce, garlic, allspice, chili powder, thyme, cinnamon, cayenne, and black pepper until combined. Add the pork, turning to coat, and marinate it in the refrigerator for at least 6 hours, turning occasionally.

3. Grill the pork, turning several times, until it is cooked through, 25 to 30 minutes. Transfer the meat to a cutting board and let it stand for 10 minutes before slicing. Serve it with the mango salsa.

Main Courses

119

Servings:
4 people

Prep time:
5 minutes
plus 1 hour
marinating

Cook time:
12 minutes

Cooking Accessory:
Cast-Iron Grill Top

Maple-Marinated Flank Steak

Maple syrup might seem like a strange ingredient to combine with beef, but it adds delightful flavor and texture as the sugar caramelizes onto the meat. For an interesting kick, add a couple tablespoons of bourbon to the marinade or a splash of soy sauce for an Asian flair. Leftover steak can be stuffed into pita bread with a creamy slaw or piled on a crusty bun with a slice of smoked cheese.

¼ cup (80 g) maple syrup

2 tablespoons (30 ml) freshly squeezed lemon juice

1 tablespoon (11 g) Dijon mustard

1 teaspoon minced garlic

1 pound (454 g) flank steak

Sea salt, to taste

Freshly ground black pepper, to taste

1. In a medium bowl, combine the maple syrup, lemon juice, mustard, and garlic. Add the beef, turning to coat. Cover and refrigerate for 1 hour.

2. Remove the steak from the marinade and season it lightly with salt and pepper. Discard the remaining marinade.

3. Grill the steak until it reaches your desired doneness, 5 to 6 minutes per side for medium.

4. Transfer the steak to a cutting board and let it rest for 10 minutes. Slice it thinly on a diagonal across the grain and serve.

Servings:
4 people

Prep time:
20 minutes

Cook time:
18 minutes

Cooking Accessory:
Cast-Iron Wok Top

Beef and Cabbage Pad Thai

Shredded cabbage takes the place of classic rice noodles in this recipe; the vegetable adds bulk and soaks up the incredible sauce. If you like a touch of heat, add a sprinkle of red pepper flakes to the sauce or serve the finished meal with a splash of hot sauce like sriracha.

For the Sauce

Juice of 1 orange

3 tablespoons (48 g) peanut butter

1 teaspoon rice vinegar

2 teaspoons (10 ml) low-sodium soy sauce

1 teaspoon honey

For the Pad Thai

1 tablespoon (15 ml) sesame oil, divided

1 pound (454 g) sirloin steak, trimmed and thinly sliced

¼ sweet onion, thinly sliced

1 teaspoon minced garlic

½ head savoy cabbage, thinly sliced

2 carrots, shredded

Chopped peanuts, for garnish

1. In a small bowl, whisk the orange juice, peanut butter, vinegar, soy sauce, and honey until well combined. Set aside.

2. Heat 1½ teaspoons of oil in the wok. Sauté the beef slices until browned, about 5 minutes. Transfer the beef to a bowl and set aside.

3. Add the remaining oil and sauté the onion and garlic until fragrant, about 3 minutes. Add the cabbage and sauté until it starts to wilt, about 6 minutes. Add the carrots and toss until softened, about 3 minutes. Add the beef, juices from the bowl, and the sauce, and toss to combine.

4. Sauté for 1 minute and serve topped with chopped peanuts.

Servings:
4 people

Prep time:
10 minutes

Cook time:
20 minutes

Cooking Accessory:
Cast-Iron Griddle Top

Gourmet Sloppy Joes

If you have a food processor or blender, your preparation time for the chopped vegetables in this dish will be considerably faster than if you have to chop everything by hand. If you want to chop using a manual method, make sure you produce a very fine dice of everything, especially the onion, to get consistency in the flavor of the dish.

1 pound (454 g) lean ground beef

1 carrot, very finely chopped

½ sweet onion, very finely chopped

½ cup (35 g) finely chopped button mushrooms

2 teaspoons (6 g) minced garlic

½ cup (245 g) tomato sauce

2 tablespoons (32 g) tomato paste

1 teaspoon red wine vinegar

Dash Worcestershire sauce

4 kaiser rolls, halved

1. Brown the beef on the griddle until it is cooked through, stirring and breaking it up with a spatula, about 7 minutes. Add the carrot, onion, mushrooms, and garlic and sauté until softened, about 5 minutes.

2. Add the tomato sauce, tomato paste, vinegar, and Worcestershire sauce, stirring to combine. Cook, stirring often, until the sauce reduces and the mixture is thick and a bit sticky, about 5 minutes.

3. Place the cut rolls along the edges of the griddle until they are lightly toasted, about 2 minutes.

4. Divide the sloppy joe mixture between the rolls and serve.

Chapter 5

Delectable Desserts and Sweets

5

Servings:
1 person

Prep time:
10 minutes

Cook time:
10 minutes

Cooking Accessory:
Cast-Iron Griddle or Grill Top

Sweet Tortilla Rollup

Tortillas are not just for savory recipes; they are the perfect vehicle for tempting sweet fillings, too. Try different combinations of ingredients to create delectable treats that can be cut into pieces and shared. Let the tortillas sit for a couple minutes if you are going to cut them, so all the filling doesn't leak out.

1 (8-inch/20-cm) flour tortilla

2 tablespoons (32 g) chocolate hazelnut spread

¼ cup (65 g) peanut butter, caramel, or white chocolate chips (your preference)

¼ cup (7.3 g) mini marshmallows

3 cookies (Oreos, graham crackers, chocolate chip), crumbled

Other desired toppings: sprinkles, caramel sauce, chopped pecans

1. Layer 2 pieces of 12-inch (30-cm) foil squares on a clean work surface.

2. Place the tortilla in the center of the foil and slather the chocolate hazelnut spread on it, leaving a 1-inch (2.5-cm) border around the edges.

3. Sprinkle the peanut butter, caramel, or chocolate chips; marshmallows; cookie crumbs; and any other desired toppings evenly over the spread.

4. Fold the nearest edge of the foil over the fillings, then fold the sides toward the center, and roll the tortilla into a cylinder.

5. Wrap the foil tightly around the tortilla and place it on the griddle or grill for about 10 minutes, turning it every few minutes.

6. Unwrap the foil and serve!

Servings:
2 people

Prep time:
15 minutes

Cook time:
10 minutes

Granola Peach Crisp

The topping on this crisp is not baked on—it is store-bought or homemade granola—but all the delightful flavors and textures are very similar. Add a scoop of vanilla ice cream or dollop of whipped cream to round out the dessert.

1½ tablespoons (21 g) butter

5 peaches, pitted and cut into ¼-inch (6-mm) slices

½ cup (115 g) brown sugar

1 teaspoon ground cinnamon

½ teaspoon ground nutmeg

¼ teaspoon ground ginger

¼ teaspoon ground cloves

1 cup (100 g) homemade or premade granola

1. Melt the butter on the griddle and add the peach slices. Sauté the peaches until they soften, about 5 minutes.

2. Add the brown sugar, cinnamon, nutmeg, ginger, and cloves and sauté until the peaches begin to caramelize, about 5 minutes more.

3. Scoop the peaches into 2 bowls and top with the granola.

4. Serve as is or with vanilla ice cream.

Delectable Desserts and Sweets

131

Servings:
2 people

Prep time:
10 minutes

Cook time:
10 minutes

Cooking Accessory:
Cast-Iron Griddle or Grill Top

Campfire Banana Boats

Who first decided to stuff ripe bananas with chocolate and marshmallows, wrap them in foil, and throw the package into a campfire to cook? That person is owed heaps of thanks! The soft fruit and gooey, melted filling are best eaten with a spoon.

2 medium unpeeled ripe bananas

¼ cup (44 g) dark or semisweet chocolate chips

¼ cup (7.3 g) mini marshmallows

2 tablespoons (10 g) shredded coconut

2 graham crackers, crushed

1. Cut the bananas lengthwise through the skin about three-quarters of the way through. Open up a pocket for the other ingredients.

2. Tear off 2 12-inch (30-cm) squares of foil and place 1 banana in the center of each.

3. Evenly divide the chocolate chips, marshmallows, coconut, and graham crackers between the bananas, stuffing them carefully into the banana openings. Crimp the foil around the bananas to enclose.

4. Place the bananas on the griddle or grill and cook until the fillings are gooey and the banana is warmed through, about 10 minutes.

5. Serve.

Servings:
4 people

Prep time:
15 minutes

Cook time:
30 minutes

Cooking Accessory:
Cast-Iron Grill Top

Rustic Baked Apples

Sometimes the simplest dessert is the most satisfying. The luscious crunchy, lightly spiced apple filling in this recipe is hard to resist, especially surrounded by soft, sweet fruit. You can prepare this recipe ahead and keep the apples wrapped in the refrigerator for up to three days, even if the cored section browns. Don't worry, you won't see any brown spots once the apples are baked.

4 medium apples

¼ cup (28 g) chopped pecans

3 tablespoons (42 g) butter

¼ cup (60 g) brown sugar

2 teaspoons (4.6 g) ground cinnamon

½ teaspoon ground nutmeg

1. Core the apples, leaving the bottom intact, if possible.

2. In a small bowl, combine the pecans, butter, sugar, cinnamon, and nutmeg.

3. Evenly divide the pecan mixture between the apples, pushing the mixture into the core area.

4. Wrap each apple in aluminum foil, creating a sealed packet. Place the apples on the grill and cook, turning several times, until the apples are tender, about 30 minutes depending on the size of the apples.

5. Let the apples cool for 10 minutes, open the packets carefully, and enjoy!

Servings:
4 people

Prep time:
15 minutes

Cook time:
5 minutes

Cooking Accessory:
Cast-Iron Wok Top

Banana Fritters

Some banana fritter recipes are messy to make, dipping fruit chunks in batter and frying them. This recipe is similar to a traditional Indonesian preparation where mashed banana flavors the batter, which is scooped or piped directly into the oil. Less mess, and all the flavor! Be extra careful with the heat of the deeper oil over the fire, and let it cool before discarding.

4 medium overripe bananas

½ cup (120 ml) milk

2 large eggs

2 cups (250 g) all-purpose flour

2 teaspoons (9.2 g) baking powder

½ teaspoon ground cinnamon

½ teaspoon sea salt

¼ teaspoon ground nutmeg

Vegetable or canola oil, for frying

Confectioner's sugar, for dusting

1. In a medium bowl, mash the bananas (a bit lumpy is fine).

2. Add the milk and eggs, stirring to combine.

3. In a small bowl, whisk the flour, baking powder, cinnamon, salt, and nutmeg.

4. Add the dry ingredients to the banana mixture and stir until just combined.

5. Heat 1½ inches (3.8 cm) of oil in the wok to between 350ºF and 370ºF (177ºC and 188ºC).

6. Working in batches, drop the batter by tablespoons into the oil—do not overcrowd!—and cook until the fritters are golden brown. Flip them and fry until both sides are golden and the fritters are cooked through, about 5 minutes.

7. Transfer the fritters to a paper towel–lined plate to drain and repeat until all the batter is used.

8. Dust the fritters generously with confectioner's sugar and serve.

Servings:
8 brownies

Prep time:
15 minutes

Cook time:
30 minutes

Cooking Accessory:
Cast-Iron Griddle Top

"Baked" Fudgy Brownie

Brownies are a food group, or should be. Three types of chocolate combine in this version, and strangely, it is not overly sweet due in part to the addition of espresso powder. Cut the brownies into small bite-size pieces for a decadent snack or serve large squares with vanilla ice cream for a delightful dessert.

Nonstick baking spray

⅓ cup (75 g) butter, room temperature

½ cup (100 g) granulated sugar

¼ cup (60 g) brown sugar

2 large eggs

1 teaspoon vanilla extract

½ cup (63 g) all-purpose flour

⅓ cup (40 g) cocoa powder

½ teaspoon espresso powder

¼ teaspoon baking powder

¼ teaspoon sea salt

½ cup (87.5 g) dark chocolate chips

¼ cup (44 g) white chocolate chips

1. Lightly spray a deep 8-inch-square (20-cm-square) baking dish with baking spray.

2. In a medium bowl, cream the butter and sugars with an electric hand mixer or a whisk until light and fluffy. Add the eggs and vanilla and beat until well blended.

3. Add the flour, cocoa powder, espresso powder, baking powder, and salt and beat until just combined.

4. Stir in the chocolate chips and spoon the batter into the prepared baking dish.

5. Place another baking dish upside down on the griddle and the brownie-filled baking dish on top of it. Cover with a large disposable roasting pan and "bake" the brownies until a toothpick inserted in the center comes out clean, about 30 minutes.

6. Cool in the baking dish and serve.

Servings:
4 people

Prep time:
15 minutes

Cook time:
30 minutes

Cooking Accessory:
Cast-Iron Grill Top

Grilled Blueberry Peach Pie

Yes, you can make pie on a grill with a little ingenuity and a cover or disposable baking tray. It is a free-form creation rather than a proper pie, but equally delicious with a crisp golden crust and bursting with fruit. You can try any type of fruit in place of the blueberries and peaches, so play around with your favorite choices.

2 cups (290 g) fresh blueberries

2 peaches, pitted and thinly sliced

½ cup (100 g) granulated sugar, plus more for dusting (if desired)

2 tablespoons (16 g) cornstarch

1 tablespoon (15 g) lemon juice

½ teaspoon ground cinnamon

1 premade piecrust

1 teaspoon milk

1. In a medium bowl, toss the berries, peaches, sugar, cornstarch, lemon juice, and cinnamon.

2. Loosen the piecrust in its disposable foil pie plate keeping it intact and pile the fruit mixture in the center.

3. Brush the edges with the milk and sprinkle with more granulated sugar, if you desire.

4. Place an inverted disposable 8-inch-square (20-cm-square) baking dish (see Note) on the grill and set the pie on top. Cover with a large roasting pan and "bake" until the piecrust is golden and cooked through and the filling is bubbly, about 30 minutes.

5. Remove the pie from the grill and let it cool before cutting it into quarters and serving.

Note: It is best to use a disposable aluminum foil baking dish for this recipe.

Servings:
8 cookie bars

Prep time:
10 minutes plus refrigeration

Cook time:
20 minutes

Cooking Accessory:
Cast-Iron Griddle Top

Chocolate Chip Cookies

If you enjoy crispy cookies rather than cakey ones, this recipe will soon be a regular campfire activity. The inside of the cookies stays gooey and they are fabulous served warm off the griddle or cooled for a later treat. Change up the chocolate chips for other chips (white chocolate, anyone?) or add nuts like pecans, depending on your preference.

1 cup (225 g) butter, room temperature

¾ cup (150 g) granulated sugar

¼ cup (60 g) brown sugar

⅓ cup (80 ml) milk

1 large egg

1 teaspoon vanilla extract

2 cups (250 g) all-purpose flour

1½ teaspoons baking soda

1 teaspoon sea salt

2 cups (350 g) semisweet chocolate chips

Nonstick cooking spray

1. In a medium bowl, cream the butter and sugars with an electric hand mixer or a whisk until light and fluffy, about 2 minutes.

2. Beat in the milk, egg, and vanilla until well blended.

3. Add the flour, baking soda, and salt and mix with a spoon until just combined. Add the chocolate chips and stir.

4. Transfer the dough to a piece of plastic wrap, fold it up, and refrigerate until firm.

5. Lightly spray an 8-inch-square (20-cm-square) disposable baking dish with cooking spray and press the cookie batter into it, creating one large layer of cookie dough.

6. Place another 8-inch-square (20-cm-square) baking dish upside down on the griddle and place the baking dish with the cookie dough on top. Top with a deep roasting pan and cook until the cookie is brown on the bottom and lightly browned on top, about 15 to 20 minutes.

7. Cut into 8 equal pieces and serve warm.

Note: It is best to use a disposable aluminum foil baking dish for this recipe.

Servings:
However many
you want

Prep time:
5 minutes

Cook time:
1 minute

Cooking Accessory:
Roasting Sticks

Classic S'mores, Plus Variations

S'mores are a staple campfire dessert: simple, scrumptious, and created with a roasting stick and minimal ingredients. Although the original combination—graham crackers, chocolate, and toasted marshmallow—is perfection, there are many other tasty combinations out there. Branch out with unique ingredients to create your own signature favorite. You can even try crispy bacon in your s'mores; the salty plus sweet combination is spectacular.

Cookies (graham crackers, arrowroot biscuits, peanut butter cookies, chocolate chip cookies, ginger cookies, wafer cookies, or stroopwafels)

Chocolate (dark chocolate, semisweet chocolate, milk chocolate, white chocolate, peanut butter cups, peppermint patties, orange-flavored chocolate) or chocolate spread

Marshmallows

Extras: caramel sauce, lemon curd, peanut butter, caramels, chopped nuts, M&M's, shredded coconut, rice cereal treats, fresh berries (at Solo, we particularly like raspberry s'mores), banana slices, or jam

1. Take 2 cookies and place any type of chocolate on one, or spread the cookie with chocolate spread or any of the extras.

2. Skewer a marshmallow on a roasting stick and toast it until golden brown over the Solo Stove.

3. Place the toasted marshmallow on the chocolate, add any extras, and cover with the remaining cookie.

4. Press the cookies together gently and wait a couple seconds for the warm marshmallow to melt the fillings.

5. Repeat!

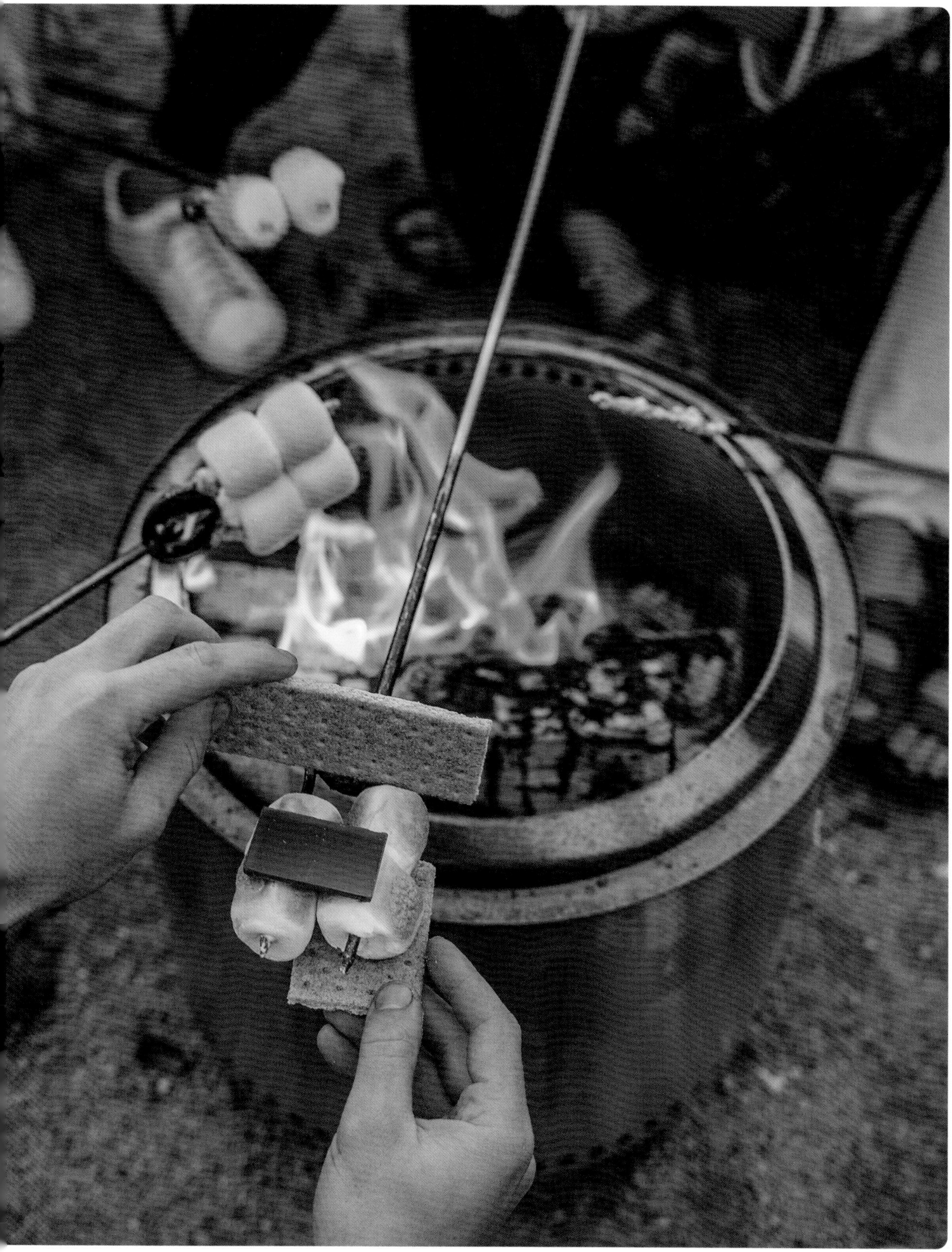

Servings:
24 mini donuts

Prep time:
30 minutes
plus rising time

Cook time:
2 minutes

Cooking Accessory:
Cast-Iron Wok Top

Homestyle Donuts

The trick to making donuts over a campfire is monitoring the oil carefully so it stays at the correct temperature, between 325°F and 350°F (163°C and 177°C). Keep checking it and adding small pieces of wood when required. These golden beauties can be dipped in chocolate icing or dusted with confectioner's sugar instead of the glaze.

For the Donuts

1 tablespoon (9.3 g) active dry yeast

¼ cup (60 ml) warm water

½ cup (120 ml) warm milk

¼ cup (55 g) melted butter

¼ cup (50 g) granulated sugar

1 large egg

½ teaspoon sea salt

2½ cups (313 g) all-purpose flour, divided

Vegetable oil for frying

For the Glaze

1 cup (120 g) confectioners sugar

2 tablespoons (30 ml) whole milk

½ teaspoon vanilla extract

(Recipe instructions on page 148)

(continued from page 147)

1. In a large bowl, combine the yeast and water, letting it stand for 5 to 10 minutes.

2. Add the milk, butter, sugar, egg, and salt, whisking to combine. Add 2 cups (250 g) of flour and mix using a wooden spoon.

3. Add the remaining flour, using your hands to create a shaggy well-mixed dough.

4. Transfer the dough to a large, greased bowl, cover it with a clean kitchen towel, and place it in a warm draft-free place to rise until doubled, about 1½ hours.

5. Turn the dough out onto a flour-dusted work surface and roll it out until it is ½-inch (1.3-cm) thick. Use a small donut cutter or a small round cookie cutter to create the donuts. You should have 24 mini donuts. Let them stand for 15 minutes before frying.

6. Heat 2 inches (5 cm) of oil in the wok to about 350°F (177°C). Working in batches, carefully drop the donuts into the oil and fry them until golden on the bottom, about 1 minute. Flip them over and fry until golden on the second side and cooked through, about 1 minute more.

7. Transfer the donuts to a paper towel–lined rack or plate.

8. Repeat with the remaining donuts.

9. While the donuts are cooling, make the glaze. In a small bowl, whisk the sugar, milk, and vanilla until smooth. Dip the donuts into the glaze and serve warm or at room temperature.

About
Solo Stove

Since our beginnings in 2010, Solo Stove has been a trailblazer, redefining the outdoor living landscape. Our fire pits kindle enduring memories, opening space for togetherness and shared experiences. We ignite the flames of connection, where laughter echoes and bonds deepen. With Solo Stove, every outdoor gathering becomes a cherished moment in the open space.

Solo Stove is the cornerstone brand of Solo Brands, a company headquartered in Dallas, Texas. Our iconic stainless steel, virtually smokeless fire pits are enjoyed by a loyal and rapidly growing community of enthusiasts worldwide on patios, in backyards, and along trails and in campsites in the great outdoors. The pits have many uses, and cooking snacks and meals on the pits is an increasingly popular one among owners. In recognition of this, we now offer a full line of cooking surfaces and accessories for use with our fire pits, as well as other

food-centered product lines such as camp stoves and pizza ovens. As cooking has grown in importance among Solo Stove enthusiasts, the need for a book devoted to fire pit cooking has become clear. As a result, we at Solo Stove have partnered with The Quarto Group and with chef, recipe developer, and food writer Michelle Anderson to create this collection of fireside-friendly recipes. From everyone at Solo Stove, here's to even more lasting memories—and incredible meals enjoyed together around the fire pit.

Recipe Index by Solo Stove Accessory

Cast-Iron Grill Top

Cast-Iron Wok Top

Roasting Sticks

Index